THE GODS
MUST BE US

When Fiction Becomes A Miracle

Dennis N. Clegg, PhD

BALBOA.
PRESS

A DIVISION OF HAY HOUSE

Balboa Press books may be ordered through booksellers or by contacting:

Balboa Press
A Division of Hay House
1663 Liberty Drive
Bloomington, IN 47403
www.balboapress.com
1 (877) 407-4847

Because of the dynamic nature of the Internet, any web addresses or links contained in this book may have changed since publication and may no longer be valid. The views expressed in this work are solely those of the author and do not necessarily reflect the views of the publisher, and the publisher hereby disclaims any responsibility for them.

The author of this book does not dispense medical advice or prescribe the use of any technique as a form of treatment for physical, emotional, or medical problems without the advice of a physician, either directly or indirectly. The intent of the author is only to offer information of a general nature to help you in your quest for emotional and spiritual well-being. In the event you use any of the information in this book for yourself, which is your constitutional right, the author and the publisher assume no responsibility for your actions.

Any people depicted in stock imagery provided by Thinkstock are models, and such images are being used for illustrative purposes only. Certain stock imagery © Thinkstock.

Printed in the United States of America.

ISBN: 978-1-5043-2596-7 (sc)
ISBN: 978-1-5043-2598-1 (hc)
ISBN: 978-1-5043-2597-4 (e)

Library of Congress Control Number: 2014923007

Balboa Press rev. date: 1/20/2015

Love is the Healer LLC

loveisthehealer.com
thegodsmustbeus.com
facebook.com/LoveIsTheHealer

DEDICATION

Oneness

all inclusive—no exclusions

AUTHOR'S GRATITUDE

Each time the book comes back for me to review the editing, I am more amazed than ever. I am grateful for moments when I forget my little separate self and accessed Oneness.

I am grateful for what everyone contributes to our oneness. In that way you've contributed to this book.

I am grateful for our collective power expressed in the relaxing and dissipating of the energy of a tsunami.

I am grateful to earth angels and unseen helpers, the ones who like Susan May is a writer's cheerleader, like Anni Herring who read and commented, or to Balboa Press made up of people who love making the work of people like me shine, and of course my wife Lark Alyson Tucker Clegg who reads, comments, discusses, challenges, and supports me as I evolve with this book.

And I am grateful for every moment of my life exactly as it unfolded. I am grateful to live long enough to "get it" that almost every story about my life is long past its expiration date.

I am grateful that gratitude is abundance in action.

PREFACE

I remember an "Alfred Hitchcock" episode where a reporter wrote stories and they happened. He experimented and used it to take revenge. Once in a while, a story line morphs the writer in and out of the story. I have always loved *The Neverending Story* for the way it brings the reader into the story. I still have no intention of doing that but after over three years of trying to convince myself I couldn't tell this story publicly, I am going for it.

I am not going to bring you into the story, nor am I going in and out of the story. Yes, I lived it to write it, but that is different. What happened is that after writing part of the novel, something happened that I had no option but to apply what I was writing to a real-life global event. Here is my account. It isn't for conjecture or interpolation. "Why" isn't available. I hardly know how. I wonder if I shall ever stop shaking within, just thinking about sharing it with you.

While I originally wrote this fictional story, I was surprised how the writing diverted from my original intention to write about an "alternate reality." On March 9, 2011, I completed the first draft, but I was perplexed about what I had written. I even wondered if it was responsible to reveal that kind of information to the public.

Two days later, something happened that I struggled to reconcile. I have vacillated between wanting to keep it a secret and needing to tell the world in such a way as to emphasize this story is not about making one person special, but rather awakening others to that of which we all are, which is best expressed in a single word: "Oneness."

For over three years, I struggled to realize this story is not my private possession to be hoarded and hidden on a flash drive.

I ask you to take some time to think of yourself in this story, as if you were me, and look for what is within yourself that could have stepped into this story as if you were me. I ascribe to a story that we are together because you are within me, and I am within you, and we are within all that is, as all that is, is within us. Therefore all of the wisdom, knowledge, understanding, powers, and abilities of our collective Oneness is available to all of us without anyone being exclusive or special ... even me.

At 2:26 a.m. on March 11, 2011, I was awakened by a text message alert on my girlfriend's cell phone. There were several unusual circumstances at that moment. First of all, I do not usually watch television; a TV is not usually available, especially where I am sleeping. I could spend several days in a motel room and never turn on the television. Whenever I am hospitalized, I don't watch television.

I had gone to Nashville, Tennessee, to visit Oscar and Emily in their independent living complex. Ellen and I were spending a month together as living date experiment because she lives in Lyman, South Carolina, and I live in Sedona, Arizona. Our dating involved short visits and many telephone conversations before March 2011, when we began living together.

One of Ellen's sisters lived in Hawaii. I spoke with her via cell phones a couple of times, but we never met. The text alert had come from her.

The message was brief; it said, "A tsunami is headed for Hawaii."

After Ellen read the message out loud, I got out of bed and turned the television on. The news channel showed images of a tsunami hitting northern Japan. As it turned out, these would be the only images the world would see for over twelve hours, as it soon became dark in Japan. It would be midafternoon in the eastern United States before the images of damage in Japan were revealed.

The news channel I was watching shifted from repeating the brief images to a scientific prediction of what would follow the major earthquake and tsunami in the entire Pacific Ocean. The tsunami was moving at more than five hundred miles an hour, just under the speed of a cruising commercial jetliner. It was estimated some islands of the

Pacific would be completely washed over. All of Hawaii was evacuated to high ground, leaving only cameras in the darkness of night to show the advent of the anticipated tsunami. Scientists predicted the angle at which the tsunami would hit Hawaii; it was expected to curl around and impact different parts of the islands. Scientists were quite certain the entire western coastlines of North and South America would be devastated.

Ellen wanted to go back to sleep and asked me to turn the television off. Soon I did.

I lay there on the bed on my stomach, something I rarely do, unless I am sick. I do not remember what was going on with my body. I kept thinking about what I had just seen and what was expected to happen. I thought about what I had written just two days before. I am a practitioner of dowsing as well as a student of energy healing (along with other forms of alternative healing). I was coming to understand quantum physics in deeply powerful ways. I thought about how I had written about dealing with another manifestation of energy; the energy of a shock wave being carried through water was a similar state of unusual energy.

I knew something must be done, and I struggled for about an hour with all of the conditioning and internal programming that says that I am small and inadequate and unable and, therefore, relegated to being a victim of the forces of nature.

Yet I knew this was not true. In 1990, my friend Steffani told me we could make clouds disappear. Once I learned it was possible, sure enough, I made clouds disappear. A while later, I told my son Aaron about making clouds disappear, and he told me he could make the wind blow. So I told him, "Learn to make the wind stop blowing. It would sure make a lot of outdoor activities nicer if you could stop the wind from blowing."

So a few days later, we were boating on Huntington Reservoir in central Utah. The wind was making it unpleasant for boating, so I asked Aaron if he could stop it. And he did. A while later, the wind came up again. Once again, I asked him to stop the wind. He did so. This happened several times throughout the day.

I also found that when I told children they could make clouds disappear and demonstrated it for them, without exception, they all made clouds disappear.

Eventually, I wanted to find out if I could make clouds appear. And yes, it was possible. Once, when I was feeling low and wanted a reminder that I was more than the way I was feeling, I intended to make a cloud appear over Mingus Mountain in Arizona; a large and ferocious-looking thundercloud soon appeared. I quickly made it disappear and pondered how the energy of the cloud was an expression of my inner state of being. I realized that more consciousness was needed when making clouds appear.

There are instances in which people have made rain happen where it was needed, but it did not come in moderation; those who brought it about did not know how to stop rain when it was enough. The problem is that when we desperately want rain, we do not think about the intensity we put into bringing rain, nor do we include limitations in our requests. So the intensity expresses exactly how it was put out.

It has been quite useful to be able to have blustery winds go calm for things like taking off or landing an airplane.

As I lay there, I realized I had written information that without practice, the words were nothing but theorizing. I also knew that I was being called upon to do something that all the conditioning, programming, and beliefs of my life argued against. I did not know I could, and I did not know I could not, but there would be no answer to the question of whether I could if I did not step into the role I was being pressed into. I needed to do what I knew.

With the tsunami's wave traveling at over 500 MPH, I had no idea if islands had already been washed over, nor did I know how many islands were in jeopardy. There was not time to procrastinate or think about it further. I would not be able to live with myself if I did not act with everything I knew possible.

There were no spells or incantations. There were no ceremonies or rituals. I had no dowsing tools with me. I had no prayers or remembered lists of celebrity angels to call in. All I had was what I knew. I had delayed enough. It was time to act.

So in the darkness of a windowless room in Nashville, with the entire Pacific being dark and an enormous wave of energy pushing toward coastlines in its path, I applied what I know to make the energy of that enormous tsunami relax and dissipate.

After I did what I knew, I lay on my side, spooning Ellen, and fell into a restful sleep.

The next morning, we went to Oscar and Emily's apartment for breakfast, and I told them what was going on in Japan. We turned on their television to a live feed of the arrival of the tsunami in Hawaii. The exact time this tsunami would arrive had been scientifically calculated. We watched in anticipation. I was unsure if what I had experienced in the night was nonsense or something significant. As I waited for the cameras to show the rising water, part of me wanted it all to happen just as the scientists predicted, so I could be free of dealing with what it might mean in my life if somehow the energy of that tsunami did relax and dissipate.

It is a matter of history now. How quickly the world forgot; I did not hear any scientists explain how the energy of that tsunami in the Pacific had disappeared. The news went to the damaged nuclear power plants.

After you've completed reading the book, you'll join me in wonder. The tsunami only hit Japan. That is a historical fact. There is absolutely no way of knowing for certain what happened to the energy of that tsunami. There is no final authority that can definitively tell what happened to its power. I know only what happened and why I took action.

This book discusses possibilities, raises questions, and leaves you to ponder what your answers might be.

I look forward to meeting with you in wonder.

CHAPTER 1

Teuton was aware of the pulsing of his heart and muffling the sound of his breathing as he made his way carefully, where in the summer, was a path that would take him to the road near the bottom of the canyon. He could feel the tingling through his body in a state of hypervigilance. The snow had a sound as it gently fell amongst the pines and bare limbs of quaking aspen trees in the darkness of early evening. The snow boots on his feet shuffled through eight inches of freshly fallen powdery snow. He extended his awareness as much as possible to sense any changes, any movement, or any sounds that might give him warning that an avalanche might suddenly descend from nowhere to engulf him, breaking bones with each twist and curl, and finally resting with him buried in torturous pain unable to do anything to get precious air to breathe. This was a time for complete and utter awareness of all his senses, hoping at the least he might have some warning before a relentlessly sliding avalanche would engulf him, rendering him helpless to a smothering death.

Less than an hour before, Teuton was wrapping up his day of work as the thermal engineer for Snowbird Village, up in the Wasatch Mountains of Utah. He was driving from the upper village to the shop, the last building on the downhill side of the lower village. His ride was the company's white GMC pickup with an aluminum shell covering his tools in the back. The order came over Teuton's radio, commanding everyone to get inside of a building, because the ski patrol was predicting imminent danger of avalanche.

He'd been through the ski patrol avalanche training required for employees. They'd emphasized how important it was to obey the orders of the ski patrol. He immediately pulled into the parking lot uphill of the Inn. He didn't need to be convinced the avalanche danger was real. Already this season, there were seven deaths related to avalanches in Little Cottonwood Canyon, and Teuton saw with his own eyes an avalanche wipe out a line of traffic, as skiers were leaving the village one afternoon. It covered the cars in snow and wiped several vehicles off the road and down the slope of the bunny hill. The Inn at Snowbird was known to be one of the least likely areas to experience the eerily quiet rush of an avalanche because of a forested area on the mountainside above the Inn. When the Mormon pioneers logged the trees in the canyon, they'd created a peril that did not exist before. The precious trees that held the snow to the sides of the steep canyon could not regenerate, because the young trees were broken off by sliding snows in winter.

As Teuton walked from his truck across the bridge that goes to the fifth-story lobby of the Inn, he was thankful he had been nearby when the avalanche warning was broadcast. It was a safe place to wait until the ski patrol lifted their restriction. The uphill wall of the building was thick, heavily reinforced concrete, without windows, and there was ample space for an avalanche to pile against the building. The design hadn't been put to the test.

As he entered, he greeted friends and joined in conversation with others around the fireplace. They discussed where avalanches usually zip down the rugged steep canyon walls. They mused how the Inn was considered one of the two safest buildings in Snowbird Village.

Suddenly Jack, the Inn manager, who was standing at the front desk opposite the doors, let out a shriek. His panicked voice made it hard for Teuton to understand what he was saying, but the danger in his voice was clear. Teuton immediately sprang from his chair and bolted toward the doors. He stopped suddenly with the realization that snow was quietly rushing in through both sets of double doors, into the lobby, and surrounding his feet! Except for the sound of Jack's voice, there was little to be heard. The doors even opened quietly.

The Great Salt Lake causes a lake effect in winter; it creates powdery light snow, with less moisture. Utah skiing is famous for powdery snow. One of its characteristics is that it muffles sounds more than wet and heavy snow. When Teuton realized the snow was continuing to pile against the counter, he knew he had taken exactly the wrong action in response to Jack's warning. He froze that instant, heart pumping so hard he felt as if he might explode. What little of his body was exposed through the layers of winter clothing was as white as the snow quietly rushing through the doors.

Teuton regained his composure, spun about, and retreated toward the fireplace.

The avalanche had buried the highway, covered the resort road that descended to the Inn's parking lot, pounced upon all of the vehicles in the parking area in front of the bridge (including Teuton's truck), and continued across the bridge through the double set of double-glass doors, finally dammed by the front counter. Snow piled on the bridge to maximum capacity and then fell over the railings, while the remaining snow of the avalanche continued down the mountainside, piling against the windowless concrete uphill side of the Inn.

By the time the ski patrol announced the lock-down was over and people were free to leave the building, it was dark. There was no hope of Teuton continuing his drive, which would've taken him to the highway and then back up the canyon on another resort road toward the Snowbird Center, to turn again down the road at the bottom of the canyon to the well-sheltered maintenance garage. The garage was another safe area, protected by the shape of the canyon and a good stand of tall and strong trees. The Inn was the closest building to the shop. Teuton had scouted the trail in the summer between the buildings. Even though the trail was now under several feet of snow, Teuton thought he could follow it to punch out his time card and walk to the Snowbird Center to catch a bus back to the valley below.

Teuton stood at the bottom of the Inn, on the downhill side, in the safety of the leeward protection of the building. Steam rose from the hot tub and heated pool, mixing with the fresh snow steadily falling. From here, he would walk through a forested area of quaking aspen, pine, and fir trees to meet the road at the bottom of the canyon.

He didn't realize he could stay in the safety of the Inn for the night. His only thought was the loss of his vehicle, which only inconvenienced him rather than stopped him.

Teuton was an adventurer who would challenge himself to move through what he feared. He wasn't into drugs of any sort, but his former wife accused him of getting high on his own adrenaline. Danger had an attraction for him, because when danger was present, Teuton became utterly focused in the moment; like a meditation, he had refreshing relief from the usual stream of thoughts he'd become more aware of as he explored meditation. While in intensity and danger, he was at his best and loved the challenge of being alert, intense, and acting spontaneously, as he would weave his way through the same experiences that maimed or killed others.

One of Teuton's favorite activities was piloting an airplane. At the controls of an airplane, he didn't think of other things. His mind was at rest more easily than sitting in silent meditation, because in the danger and responsibility of the moment, the mind's stream of thoughts was absent, giving him a precious mental rest. Teuton felt secure if he was in control, for he trusted his ability to do the right thing if a situation got intense.

Teuton didn't want to tell anyone about his frequent suicidal thoughts. Some secrets aren't to be admitted. He'd struggled with depression a great deal in his life, and if anything, moments of feeling really alive, with humor and intensity, could stimulate his brain to counteract the sadness that he so often sank into. A few times earlier in life, he'd done things that were reckless, even uttering, "Death, I dare you!" as he started into peril. He carried a certain amount of guilt and confusion about others he knew who died in accidents; something, someone, always seemed to miraculously prevent harm coming to him. He had skirted Vietnam and carried the pain of all his friends who went there and didn't return. Perhaps by creating circumstances in which he challenged death, he could reconcile the unfairness of his living on. His guilt only increased, as he was confused about his self-worth, being compared to the many times he knew his death had been prevented. It said to him his life was important and was being preserved for something, but he took it as a nemesis more than being in gratitude and changing what of himself was out of coherence with how he had been protected.

Just as a young diver often stands on the high dive platform, building the courage to jump into the pool below, Teuton stood until he felt the courage to begin this walk, with his small mini-flashlight clutched in his mitten. With the first few steps, he felt a sense of relief that the decision was made and he was on his way. For a few moments, he felt a charge of energy throughout his body for the victory over himself to move forward.

After a while, Teuton was unsure where he was. He wasn't even certain that he was on the trail he thought he was taking. The trail was only a memory, with many layers of snowfall covering it since its last use before the snows began. It was dark, and the snow kept falling. His flashlight reflected off the snowflakes, as if to blind him from seeing further. In the moonless night, without it, he wouldn't see anything at all.

Once while on a hunting trip, in the snow of morning daylight, when the others were unsure, Teuton led the way. He had confidence in his gift for being well oriented. After hiking for some time, his hunting party arrived at footprints in the snow. Teuton naturally announced there were other hunters in the area, but one of his companions pointed out they had made a complete circle to their own footprints. As they followed the footprints, Teuton became even more shaken up with realization that he had hiked in a circle, even in a narrow canyon that defined their position. It was the classic textbook case of how people become lost. He couldn't believe he could make such a mistake.

Tonight, he was walking slightly downhill in a forested area. If he continued to follow the slope downhill, he would get to the road that went along the bottom of the canyon. However, memory of his fallibility sent chills of fright throughout his body. It was then he considered turning back, but his ego had to prove he could find his way, for he knew he was surrounded by buildings and roads. Walking straight in any direction would lead to something, so he couldn't conceive of getting lost. But could he walk straight—not in a circle—even if he turned around now? Once before, he thought he had walked a straight line in a snowfall. He failed the test once.

In the subtle noise of softly falling snow adding to the powdery coating of new snow everywhere, Teuton wondered if he were now in an area of vulnerability. *Could an avalanche blast its way to the creek at the bottom of the canyon?* He did all he could not to make a sound, for he had previously heard the approach of an avalanche and wanted to have warning rather than being taken completely by surprise. He didn't rush, for he knew acting hastily in fear could bring an accident of its own. He could fall, be injured, be trapped in a freezing tomb, where he may not be discovered until spring thaw. Only a year before, a missing person was discovered in the same area when the snows melted in spring.

He had a foreboding feeling something was about to happen.

Teuton felt like a hunted animal with a predator he didn't know stalking him. He felt deeply the vulnerability of the predicament he had chosen. He was supremely focused, in a state of hyper awareness, ready to respond with limited options where the season's snowfall had exceeded ten feet. The adventure challenged him deeply, and he loved it. It fed his masculinity to walk tall in the face of being in harm's way, without witnesses or the distraction of fanfare. When facing challenges, Teuton believed in his aloneness. He didn't like being part of a chain that might be broken at a weak link. Yet there was a deeper shadow, hoping no one would know, so no one would be there to save him. Perhaps this time, his death would not be prevented.

There was every possibility of tripping over one of the many forest deadfalls; his boots were designed to keep his feet warm, not for walking. The creek was hidden under the deep snow at the bottom of the canyon, and because the water originated from a cave, it continued to flow. Falling through the encrusted snow that arched over the running water would be even worse than an avalanche, for it would likely be a long time before he was discovered. Teuton was accustomed to working alone, and moving alone; no one knew what he was doing or where or when. At least an avalanche would be probed for the possibility of having swept someone into it. Falling into the creek might go undiscovered.

Teuton knew he would keep a cool head to reduce the possibility of an accident. He didn't know if there was some kind of controlling force purposely causing avalanches with the intent to punish certain people, but his shadow self wanted it to be so.

His thoughts had wandered, his focus was compromised, and for just a moment, his balance was off. He felt as if he were passing through a thin membrane as he struggled to find his balance; an unfamiliar force seemed to be tripping him up.

Suddenly, Teuton was in an entirely different place; there was no snow, no cold. It was warm and humid. He was bewildered. What had just happened? Had he suddenly died, not conscious of how? He struggled in his disorientation. His instinct was to fight. He didn't know what he was fighting, for the forces that had taken him against his will didn't offer anything tangible to fight with.

He felt a chill racing up and down his body. Helplessness terrified him. He wasn't aware of seeing anything but blurs of light as he was rapidly kicking his legs and thrashing about with his arms, but that didn't solve anything. His kinesthetic nature had to surrender to seeing and hearing. He became aware he was lying on the ground. There was sunlight and vegetation, but he couldn't make anything out; it was all a blur. The feel of the place was calming. He began to evaluate his predicament.

Did an avalanche get me? He thought. *Why wasn't there some drama, some trauma before I left my body? This isn't at all like the near-death accounts I've read.*

He tried to take in this strange happening, for this might be a dream. It might disappear at any moment. He had been taught that if you don't have a memory of how you got somewhere, it was a dream. Therefore, this must be a dream. He wanted to take in and remember this one. Was this the most amazing dream his mind had ever conjured up, or was he finally able to travel somewhere in his sleep state?

He struggled to his feet and noticed his clothing was still the same, but there was no snow on him. He looked around the area but couldn't clearly see anything. He felt cheated. Where was the tunnel with the light? Where was the special person to greet him? This didn't fit what people said who experienced death and came back.

With his blurry vision, he noticed some people dressed in shorts and light shirts standing around; some looked at him, but most did not.

"Where am I?" he demanded, unable to remain composed.

Others started to move around as if to move away from him. This annoyed Teuton even more. If this was heaven, it wasn't very happy.

Someone touched his shoulder. He wheeled around to see a large young man with soft, concerned eyes, very fit, very muscular, and able to deal with a struggle. The choice was clearly Teuton's. He could give up fighting or struggle with this formidable young man. He was aware he still had all his winter gear on, and he began to feel hot. Whatever was going on, he needed to remove his heavy clothing.

Two women came up to him from behind. They moved with gentle confidence as they helped him out of his clothing. He reluctantly accepted their assistance and was soon down to his thermal underwear; he was still too hot, but he was glad to be covered.

The young man motioned for Teuton to follow him. He did, hoping it would lead to answers. No one else had spoken. He was led to a bench, and the man simply motioned for him to sit. As Teuton sat on the bench, he looked up to see the others walking past, not paying him any attention.

The muscular young man went to the office to report Teuton's arrival. He spoke to Sequoia, the creator and leader of the place.

"Sequoia," the muscular young man said, "we seem to have attracted the wrong person. This man isn't ready to be here. He's lifetimes away. His energy is disturbed, and when he arrived, he was fighting ... with nothing."

"I will go meet him," Sequoia said. "I know him deeply. If he is not so closed down and resistant, he will begin to remember. Don't be concerned. He may challenge us, but as he remembers who he is, an amazing man will emerge."

Teuton felt calm. Nature had always been his solitude. He didn't trust people much.

He noticed a flowing grace, moving a simple yet elegant gown. He followed from the feet upward to see if he recognized the person coming toward him. His vision was blurred. Her features were not discernable to him. He needed to trust her at least enough to get some answers. He needed some information, any information at all.

"May I sit by you?" Sequoia said in a truly feminine voice that exuded strength and confidence. "Perhaps your transition here was unpleasant?"

"How did I die?" Teuton muttered in disbelief.

"You didn't die," Sequoia responded gently.

"Then why am I not in my life?" he muttered argumentatively. "This is clearly something else. I'm not free to be where I was. The grim reaper didn't even show his face. Okay, so I didn't go lights out, I still exist, but I'm not in my life any more, so this must be the afterlife."

"Your lifetime at Snowbird is still under way. Do you want me to help you understand what happened?" Sequoia asked, speaking with a sternness in her voice that was establishing boundaries with him.

"Give me your best shot!" he replied defiantly.

"Perhaps you haven't been alone long enough. I can return when you have regained your composure and are ready to understand where your life is right now. You won't know until you can accept what is right here and now. As long as you are intent on believing things should be different than they are, we can't talk." She spoke gently yet firmly so he would know he was not welcome to intrude upon her or this place. Then she got up from the bench and walked away.

Teuton pondered his predicament. He peeled off his thermal shirt, now sticky with sweat. He realized he still couldn't see clearly. Blurred images suggested what he was unfamiliar with. Not being able to see his surroundings clearly, he made sense of it all with what he believed, yet it wasn't helping him. He needed to open himself to seeing things as they were, not imposing his beliefs on his experience out of his discomfort with the unknown. He realized he hadn't seen anything past his beliefs yet. That wasn't much at all, especially blurred. He reasoned if this was heaven, perhaps he could really blow it and end up in hell. Just then, another man appeared with a drink and snack on a small platter.

Without saying a thing, or making any eye contact, the man placed the platter next to Teuton, turned, and walked away.

Again Teuton was alone, but the snack was tasty and welcomed. *Heaven might not be so bad if I can just stay here,* he reasoned with himself. Still, he was angry. It wasn't what it was supposed to be. He wondered if he had ended up in hell instead; it wasn't as bad as hell had been described.

"Teuton." He heard a woman's familiar voice as he felt his forearm being touched. "I see you've been resting. How are you feeling now?"

"What is going on? I mean, where am I? How did this happen?" Teuton asked more gently.

"May I sit by you?" Sequoia gently asked.

Teuton sat up to make space for her on the bench. She sat down in the space he made available. Teuton realized he liked her. She had given him time to be by himself and then returned, just as she said she would.

"My name is Sequoia," she continued. "I am the founder of this place. It is neither heaven nor hell. It is the Center for Knowing Without Knowledge.

"We're on the same plane as the lifetime you've been living; you are still alive and well in that lifetime. You can be here as long as it takes, and when you return, you'll recover from stumbling on a log and continue where you were going. Only a nanosecond-long moment of that lifetime will be lost. I've reminded you. You already knew that, and because you knew your lifetime would continue, you were upset. You also knew you would be here. You were confused, because you only know linear time. Time is a helpful idea, but it is far from how things really are."

With more friendliness in his voice, Teuton asked, "How did I get here, wherever here is?"

Sequoia giggled a little and then replied, "You're on an island in the Indian Ocean, an island of so little consequence it simply goes unnoticed. The people who have gathered here came much the same as you have. You were one of those who were transported at the speed of thought, through what you might call a portal, with no distance between where you entered and here. Space is a mysterious phenomenon. Pause for a moment to see you knew that."

Teuton closed his eyes and listened for his thoughts. There was only one, and it was without words. He knew but didn't have knowledge to remember. Already he was realizing he understood the name of her institute was true. As he opened his eyes again, he realized too that his vision was clearing. Leaves had form. Objects had borders and texture. He turned to see Sequoia. She was beautiful, and she was gazing into his eyes. He couldn't look away. He was taken by the openness and love of her being. His heart leapt within his chest. He didn't know who she was, but he knew he knew her. His hands drifted toward her. Her hands reached upward, and he realized his were meeting hers. The beauty of the place paled at the beauty of the connection he felt with her. His heart was expanding. Was she real? Was she a product of his imagination, the fulfillment of his deepest desire? She slowly smiled, a smile that furthered the awakening sense of knowing Teuton was in. He didn't know if he'd smiled first or if he smiled in return, but he knew he was unabashedly radiating his delight. Time lost relevance; there was a shift, as both remained ... open ... seeing the offering of the other, of allowing depth of exposure some people never experience in a lifetime. Safety was not possible; the exchange of deeply experiencing each other went unchecked.

Teuton knew that he knew, but he didn't know what it was that he knew. He knew she also knew, yet in that moment, all that was known was that a connection was happening, deep and familiar.

Sequoia was a scientist, an explorer of paranormal phenomenon. Deeply intuitive, her gifts enabled her to work within the unknown and be at ease with the unknowable to bring insights to others. This led to her being the founder of the Center of Knowing Without Knowledge, or C-Know.

Throughout her life, Sequoia had been looked up to and revered for her gifts, something she had mixed feelings about, until she had the inspiration to create C-Know. Sequoia learned there is no honor in being able to know things beyond common understanding with most people. She didn't want to be famous. Her family was immensely wealthy and adept at living incognito. Fame to her was not kind to those who live beyond the lifestyles and belief systems of society. Her experiences taught her that people are too resistant to what they don't understand.

Sequoia, while reluctant, felt compelled to find coherence with people to share life in extraordinary reality.

Born into privilege, she was accepted and encouraged to live her gifts. She got to attend the schools she wanted and could afford private coaching with people she wanted to learn from. She had a naturally independent nature, not rebellious, although few understand the rebellious operate from a gut energy of anger and defiance, while independent people simply know themselves and live true to themselves. There is no attachment within her to rebel against. She is simply an authentic woman. C-Know grew from her realizations, and she crafted ways to speed up the proficiencies she'd mastered so that others could master them.

Sequoia's almond-shaped eyes were deeply expressive, changing in hues of green and blue. Her features expressed character in her every thought and feeling. Her mixed-race ancestry gifted her with a smooth and glowing complexion.

Sequoia knew confidence and beauty was power and that with or without make-up, her inner beauty amplified her attractiveness. She'd experienced her beauty to be an advantage—with a lot of disadvantages. Fortunately, the modeling school she attended in her teens emphasized inner beauty and confidence, which outlasted the fleeting nature of outward beauty. With or without make-up, fashion, and poise, Sequoia valued being deeply authentic with an inner sense of right and wrong, independent of rules and laws. She opened up with those she was close to and enjoyed being real. She chose to have loved ones who intimately knew her as a real person for who and what she was ... inside.

Creating and managing C-Know for Sequoia was an opportunity for reconnecting with life in the balance, which she'd achieved before she met her husband. She still harbored moments of pain, disappointment, hurt, loss, and the anvil of self-betrayal for all she gave up for that relationship. At the time, Sequoia became lost from herself. But through becoming lost from herself and the journey of healing, she developed an awareness of who she is and how to discern and choose experiences and people she chose to connect with.

Sequoia wasn't interested in a relationship when she founded C-Know. Her needs were met through connecting deeply with others who could meet her in harmony. She was quite sure she had risen above sexuality through exploring until she no longer felt the desire for it.

Teuton was self-determining, a man who out of being deeply disillusioned with authority, was his own authority. He carried himself with confidence, as if he alone determined what others might think of him. His shoulders were broad and muscular. When he spoke, people were often convinced he knew, even if he was unsure of himself or was making a guess. His eyes hid himself to all but the very perceptive. His unusual facades appeared to be authentic because of his rebellious nature, but the energy of where he came from was in the pit of his stomach. He laughed a lot, so much so that one would think life, to Teuton, was a comic play. Yet his laughter and light-hearted exterior kept him from shadows and darkness he didn't want to acknowledge. His approach to his youth was to move on to new chapters and leave childhood behind, as if it had no impact at all on him.

Teuton's ancestry was from the American melting pot: a mix of nationalities and races, giving him a slightly darker complexion. He had hazel eyes with long eyelashes and thick brows that attracted first looks. All of his life, no matter what nation or culture he was in, people would approach him and say he reminded them of someone else. These were usually famous and accomplished people; sometimes it was just someone they were fond of. Secretly, he hoped someday people would recognize him for an accomplishment and fame of his own.

Teuton abhorred being given advice, neither inviting it nor listening to it when advice is imposed upon him. It didn't mean he couldn't use some advice, it is just that he has a deep distrust of people and intolerance of lies, yet because of what he hasn't faced and worked through, his striving to be one personality consistent and solid often did not fit the truth of the moment. What he didn't want to see, defined his blindness. His blindness hid a deeply good and gifted man.

13

Teuton also had the quality of seeing the best in people but hadn't learned to see them as real too. This set him up for self-made disappointment and anger for people not being as he wanted them to be. It wasn't that the best in them didn't exist. What he saw was real, their potentiality. Teuton had not developed an understanding that accepting the whole paradox, with all the seeming discrepancies and opposites, was completeness. He hadn't learned that when duality ended by embracing the whole, inward and outward, he wouldn't be so judging and full of anger, distrust, and fear. The macho bravado was a game he could play with the best, to his own peril.

Being schooled in science doesn't stop Teuton from sensing he is connected to something of the paranormal himself, and he too sensed an energy about the future but didn't have a real paradigm to translate that energy into accurate information.

Teuton hesitates to consider himself a scientist, for like other terms like "god" and "doctors," the word "scientist" is exploited. When people state, "Scientists say …," without being specific as to what scientist they mean, Teuton gets red in the face. He knows that scientists act just like priests, politicians, and other people on the planet: quarreling, invalidating each other, making claims that are later unfounded, and discrediting the well founded. He really feels his anger when he hears the term "scientist" misused as another label of power over the ignorant.

While Teuton tried to use many tools to know himself and resolve his inner conflicts, he was inclined to forget all he was learning and practicing when something would trigger him. Then he would cycle through guilt and shame, using self-degradation to try to motivate himself to make it past the mysterious inner barriers that prevented him from having the life he longed for.

As they sat on the bench, Sequoia felt the pain of separation between them. She remembered many lifetimes with Teuton, sharing privilege and often as politicians or royalty. She also remembered lifetimes when they dedicated themselves to developing wisdom through spiritual exploration.

In her knowing, she knew her and Teuton to be as soul-mates or twin flames destined to come together again, but Teuton made a daring choice in this lifetime: to break up a wall he didn't go beyond from lifetime to lifetime. In their love for each other, this barrier also was the reason Sequoia was determined to go onward without the possibility of Teuton holding her back. He was still in the chaos of a difficult childhood, unable to use it as it was intended because of trying so hard to move on, not accepting his earlier life as it was and pretending he came from something else.

For Teuton, looking into Sequoia's eyes and feeling the exchange in their hands meeting was like living a love dream so real, possible, and yet in his basic belief, he didn't deserve good things; he created barriers without being conscious of what he was doing. For Sequoia, it was meeting the love of lifetimes, now separate and distant. She felt the longing. She knew love existed between them. Yet she knew the chasm between them may mean lifetimes shared may have been passages, meetings of love that hadn't endured, couldn't endure his present lifetime.

This moment contained hard choices. She felt the longing of Teuton, but he was filled with a need to be rescued and saved, something he still wanted from someone else, because he hadn't discovered he could, would, and must, rescue and save himself. The draw of love was almost impossible not to surrender to. For now, Sequoia knew she must establish boundaries with Teuton. She knew her life as it was in this lifetime would add to the pain and challenges for Teuton. In this lifetime, she'd expanded from a dedicated love partner to many love partners without exclusivity. He longed for exclusive love; he also built barriers to experiencing, but he couldn't see that. He'd been torn between "Miss Right Now" and his sense that there really was a right woman for him. Somewhere in the middle, he didn't do relationships well.

He wasn't in telepathy with her, as it had been in other lifetimes. That pained her. She felt a deep sadness.

He saw pain in her eyes and felt loss of what was transpiring moments before. Tears welled up in her eyes, and she trembled as she began to cry. Teuton was confused at the change, but in judgment, he lumped her change into his perceptions of women, the perceptions that kept him lonely and unfulfilled. Their hands drifted apart. Sequoia rose to her feet, simply choked, "Excuse me," in the midst of her crying, and rushed away.

For a few moments, Teuton touched upon the love he always longed for, something that was like the North Star in his life. He wondered if his excitement and need drove her away. It wasn't the first time a woman ran away from his neediness.

He sat with his elbows on his knees, palms of his hands cradling his jaw, and fingers laying on his cheeks. His eyes were closed. Many thoughts appeared, but he couldn't make a story with them. He had no sense of what it all meant.

"Come with me," he heard a voice saying. Teuton opened his eyes to see a middle-aged man with graying hair and a well-trimmed beard hiding the sharper angles of his face. He had kind and soft eyes. Otherwise, he was much like the image Teuton saw in the mirror. The man stood with a posture of authority, not the authority over others, but the authority of knowing himself and loving what he knows. Teuton knew he could trust him, at least for now.

He followed the man to a well-kept lawn in front of a building that was blurred from his view. This troubled Teuton, but he set it aside to see what was going on near him. People were gathering and forming a circle. Teuton joined them on the circumference and the man he had followed went into the center of the circle. Teuton felt a warmth and familiarity around these people and wondered who they were.

The man addressed Teuton so the whole circle could hear. Teuton had already counted twenty-seven in the circle excluding himself. The man's voice commanded Teuton's attention.

"I am Azurah, your main guide. The others in the circle are also your guides. We are not in bodies as you are. We are in a parallel dimension, so to speak, usually not visible to those in bodies. You have been a guide to each of us when we were in bodies. We are a soul family."

At that, everyone in the circle spoke a greeting at the same time. He could not hear any of them individually, yet Teuton felt met and appreciated being greeted.

"You've earnestly desired to know truth, the ultimate truth, godly truth. We waited for you to desire and ask for it. This is what brought you into this experience. You caused this to happen. You are not a victim. People seldom are really victimized, although it is possible. You were assisted, but your request set this experience in motion."

From within the circle Azurah walked toward Teuton, finally standing in front of him.

"You've kept us busy, so there are many of us. We've had to work with you in shifts and go for rest and relaxation between shifts. We had to let certain things happen but did not allow them to go too far. Other things that would have been on a physical plane were altered to prevent your life purpose from being stopped. Your shadow, your darkness, your inner demons have been challenging. Your beliefs are so counterproductive. The conditioning and programming from the cruelty and violence, which served to break up the patterns of lifetimes, has so deeply imprinted you, we didn't know if you would ever be able to pull out of it, even with us doing all we were allowed to do."

Then Azurah moved even closer to Teuton, who flinched as if the man were a squad leader from ROTC.

He said more personally, "Luckily, you were amazing. You took a lot of damage, but you kept flying."

Then he walked around the circle counterclockwise, with his right hand extended to each individual in the circle as he walked.

As he approached Teuton again, he declared loudly, "We've saved you many times. Some you know of and have been troubled about. Most you weren't aware of. Your life has purpose, a mission. When you know and accept yourself, your life mission will blossom and release its fragrance." The man returned to standing in front of Teuton and said more softly, "This is why you're here, sir. This is your boot camp." Then he stepped backward into the circle, looked around at the others, and loudly asked, "Are you ready?" to which the others in unison shouted, "Yes sir!" He turned to Teuton and said, "I didn't hear you. Are you ready?"

"But I need to know exactly what I'm agreeing to," Teuton protested. "How can I know I'm ready if I don't know what is ahead of me?"

"From what will the future evolve if you don't trust the moment? Do you want a future of distrust to keep evolving and giving you the same kind of results to the control-freak idea you have to first know the future? What madness is this?" Azurah didn't intend to go along with Teuton at all.

Teuton was stunned. He couldn't react, he couldn't respond either. He knew he didn't know. His thoughts were trying to create a story that would make sense as he stood at the circumference of the group, helpless as a child, overwhelmed in his inadequacy. He felt chills and trembled. He wanted to cry, but somehow he couldn't. He remembered the morning of his plea to know truth. It was an odd prayer, unlike the practice of prayer he'd been taught. *Can I survive what I might have to go through for truth?* He thought. *If I know it all right now, will I have the courage to face it? I barely have courage to face what they're doing right now. But I am surviving right now.*

Azurah marched briskly up to Teuton, stopping just short of being toe-to-toe, and looked into his eyes. Teuton expected to be yelled at with drill sergeant force, but Azurah was intent on looking into his eyes; the message Teuton was hearing was not a voice; in fact, it was not in language at all. There was a deep well of love and understanding in Azurah's eyes. Teuton knew of Azurah's love and dedication to him, something he didn't think anyone could have for him. His inner language was speaking about what was happening, and Teuton was aware he was not witnessing the moment, and in that instant, he was witnessing the moment.

Something within him was melting. He felt quivering and vulnerable. The urge to run was there, but in this place, he was better off to stay in the present he was in, than to turn the next moments into panic and fear, irrationally running to moments that might unfold into unknown difficulties. This place, this moment, the awareness of his vulnerability was intense beyond what he feared being able to endure, but staying present with this was his best strategy to evolve in some safety. After all, those who were around him might offer the advantage of not being confined to physical bodies.

The urges of his mind were trying to be heard with memories, insisting the same kind of difficulties were in the future. Teuton was aware of the thoughts trying to command his attention, but he was focused on the face just inches in front of his. He must stay present! This man may do anything. With no body to prevent him, Teuton had no idea what might happen next. Escaping into the mind's hard drive of past stuff and using that to predict the future would not work here. The best choice each moment was witnessing everything he could be aware of, for in that he might flow in wherever the moment was evolving.

Uncomfortable as he sensed himself to be, Teuton broke the tension by glancing around. His vision wasn't clear, and his senses became confused. He returned to Azurah's eyes. Once again, he could sense with clarity. Azurah's eyes began to sparkle with delight, and he sensed himself beaming into a smile as if Azurah were simply a mirror of himself. Laughter broke out between them, quickly becoming more joyful and expanding into uncontrolled body movements, which only increased as the moment evolved into even more uproarious laughter. Everyone in the circle burst into laughter. Teuton couldn't stand up; he was laughing uproariously, and he helplessly fell to the ground. Tears filled his eyes, as he completely let go to the laughter, taking his whole being in a momentary expression, completely unable to think.

Teuton became aware of a new voice. He opened his eyes, and what was in focus for him was an aged man. The man was extending a hand to Teuton, as if to help him get to his feet. Teuton knew this would prove the first question about this man, the question of whether he were in a body or not. Teuton was learning not to trust his knowledge but to be as present as possible to learn what the moment, what his small portion of awareness of the vastness of the moment, might be, really be, independent of all he had learned. He reached up to join his hand in the old man's hand, and to his surprise, he was instantly standing. Yet the hand was physical. This man was indeed in a body, but how did he find himself standing? Was there a stream of moments he missed being present to? Had he gone unconscious? Was this man meeting him in abilities that were completely missing from everything Teuton learned?

Teuton's knowledge, the mental bank of his mind's hard drive of stored programs and data, was unable to interpret.

The old fellow had a wrinkled face, which reminded Teuton there was a story of his evolution told to those who could read it. Teuton perceived deep wisdom in the man. He exuded confidence and self-assurance. There were reserves of power available, with nothing to prove. Teuton wanted to know this man.

"Come with me, Master," the man said, his voice being the voice of the grandfather everyone wished they had.

The man turned and gracefully flowed with the care and precision of someone steady, calm, and capable. Teuton realized he'd been addressed as Master when he expected this man to be the master. He realized he was thinking in language as he remembered the moments already gone and was in his mind, in the past, about what he'd heard. At that moment, he was seeing the back of the man; the scene was of walking behind him, sensing some of what was happening but sensing there was a vastness he couldn't be aware of, and he realized he was in thought with language again, at which moment he was again taking in the moment.

Teuton became aware they were entering the sands of the beach; he could hear the sounds of the ocean. He looked away from the immediate scene of following the old man, but everything was unclear, and he couldn't sense with clarity what was there. In a blink, he looked at the back of the man leading the way, and the immediate area was clear; he could sense it with clarity. He felt the sand and realized his winter boots had been removed. He was barefoot. The comparison with the past was complete, until the realization he was playing a trick on himself with sensing the moment and going into the past for comparison. In the moment of witnessing that, he was aware of the scene immediately around him and his guide. Teuton was aware the old man was leading him up an outcropping of rocks. The rock was worn and smooth yet required careful attention to climb. Teuton easily stayed present with the challenge.

The old man paused and motioned to Teuton's left, saying simply, "Sit."

Teuton's clarity of sensing expanded to see the sun low in the cloudy sky; pilots are sky watchers, and he knew this would produce a dramatic sunset. Teuton loved to sit and watch the sunset, trying to be aware of all the nuances of changing light, being surprised when he couldn't take in the whole unfolding of everything going on in a sunset at once. He always missed something. Perhaps here, it would be different. He had to find out.

Teuton came back to awareness of his body. It was dark. It was like being brought back. But where was he? Why hadn't he noticed it was getting dark? Had his focus on the sunset been so exclusive he'd become the sunset, aware of nothing else? Probably so. His vision was limited, and he sensed being on the rocks, hearing the surf pounding. It was more intense now, the surf crashing on the rocks. He felt the spray of sea water on his face, becoming aware of it on his body.

He remembered the old man. He wasn't within Teuton's field of sensibility.

Sizing up the situation, Teuton realized he needed to get off the rocks and move to safety; the surf seemed to be increasingly dangerous. The only light was from the stars. Unable to see, he had to figure out how to move, where to move, and where safety was. He felt fear, and it overwhelmed him. His being accustomed to needing to know so much, and right now being unable to, may lead to great trouble (or even his demise). The old man was teaching him, but what was the lesson? From fear, he was trying to be where he wasn't, in the whole scenario of getting from the rocks being pounded by the surf to a place of safety, comfort, and food for the night. This place might have dangers he didn't know about: snakes, tigers, poisonous insects; his memory was full of possibilities and more than able to create terrors that would delight in making him their next meal. He could feel sweat rolling from his forehead into his eyes. It mixed with sea spray and stung his eyes. He realized he was wringing an imaginary wet cloth in his hands and had pulled his legs into a fetal position; his whole body was tense. His mind was racing through repertoires of past and trying to create a future story, a plan, to resolve his dilemma.

"Azurah, helpers, where are you all?" he hollered. "I need you! We've just met and you've always saved me. Help me!" He shouted, hoping they could hear above the waves crashing into the rocks.

There were no voices, no messages, no words either in stillness or thoughts. There was a loud crash, far louder than he'd been observing, and seawater splashed all over him, all around him. Was that his answer?

He found himself separating his hands and extending his legs without forethought. He was moving. He wasn't thinking about what to do, he was doing it. It was a moment happening, and he was flowing with his movements. He was trusting, but he couldn't take a moment to consider what he was trusting, to qualify his trust in any way. He was moving and sensing what was happening as it happened. It seemed as if everything was taking care of itself, happening of its own accord. The sounds were transformed into a symphony, and his movements dancing to musical expressions. He knew what to do and was acting as he knew, not knowing before acting but knowing he was acting as he acted, and the adjustments were just happening, as if every part of him knew exactly what to do at the precise moment of need. His breathing was deep and strong. Elation arose in his being with every part of him in cooperation within and without.

There was no remembering the past movements, for that would be an interruption of the flow in the moment. There was no thought of what was next, for that would distract. It was happening in concert.

"You can open your eyes now," a gentle voice told him.

He didn't realize his eyes were closed. There were torches flickering with light that danced in the trees, leaves, flowers, and fleeting insects around him. He hadn't yet seen the person who spoke. He caught view of the edge of a bench to his left. He followed to see at first a hand with a basket of fruit. Immediately, he felt his hunger. From there, he looked up to the face of a young Asian man, perhaps sixteen or seventeen years old. He was met with an approving smile that brought Teuton from his ordeal to curiosity about this meeting. Teuton wondered if this man was in body or out. While it was important to Teuton, he didn't yet know the qualities of being between incarnations and his own qualities.

The young man again spoke, saying, "When you know, you'll know you don't know. But in that knowing, you know."

Teuton was inexperienced with Zen or Tao. He had a sense that he got it but didn't understand the elusive nature of the message. Still, it imprinted in the expanding level of awareness he was opening to. Then the young man pulled a piece of fruit from the basket and reached into the basket again for a knife, which was underneath the fruit. Teuton watched with eagerness as the young man skillfully carved the piece of fruit. It was all he could do to remain receptive. He wanted to sit and then noticed he was standing next to another bench. Just as he sat, the young man offered Teuton a slice of fruit. The taste was unfamiliar. He hoped he would be offered another slice, but instead the young man picked another fruit and began preparing it. Teuton was ravenous. Waiting to be fed was unfamiliar to him. Still, he was at a disadvantage, and as difficult as it was for him, he considered it his best option to go along with whatever was happening. He was given a slice of the next fruit. This one was sweet, juicy, and delicious. He felt the juices swirling around his tongue, tantalizing his taste buds. *More of this*, Teuton thought to himself.

"All things in the right order and time," the young man said as he again reached for another fruit.

Teuton would have been pleased to eat each one completely. *Who is this kid to think he can treat me like a child? Doesn't he recognize me as his elder, more experienced and wiser? Somebody must have put him up to this. Must have been that Sequoia woman. That was a strange meeting.* Teuton's thoughts had left the moment. He looked at the young man, the basket of food, and everything in his sight was blurred again. As his vision cleared, he saw he was being offered yet another slice of fruit.

"All things in the right order and time," the young man repeated, as he reached for yet another fruit. Teuton didn't notice much about the taste of the fruit he had taken into his mouth. He was too busy thinking about wanting to take control of the situation and show the kid how he wanted to eat. He struggled between what he wanted to do and what he thought would be the best strategy. After all, he needed to go along so he would be sent back home. He needed his winter clothing and to find that portal. He had no idea where they might be. He hadn't developed a mind map of this place.

As he bit into the last slice of fruit, Teuton realized the young man had rotated the same order, one slice at a time, of the fruit. He was too preoccupied with wanting to show this kid who was the man to notice the flavors.

Then a woman came into the clearing. Teuton wasn't of a frame of mind to notice much, except she was a woman. She simply said, "I am your guide for next part of your journey. We will go to beach for the night. I will be taking care of your needs."

It was a short walk to the beach. She carried a lantern that lit the way. She selected a site, and Teuton noticed some blankets and pillows stacked neatly in the dim periphery of the lantern's light. "Please sit, Teuton." He sat. "In a little time, your body will begin cleansing toxins. They will be coming out of your pores, you will be passing toxins, and you may be purging toxins. Do not be frightened. I will be with you. I will take good care of you. I have plenty of water. The moon will soon come, and we will wash in the sea. Just let your actions be natural. Speak, shout, yell, cry, laugh; whatever is natural as it needs to happen. Your experience will be unique. You are safe; I will take good care of you."

"So Mr. 'All Things in the Right Order and the Right Time' was giving me fruits to mix in the right way in my body?" Teuton asked.

"Yes, that way we make the medicine effective for you."

"You people just do whatever you want with me. You haven't informed me, I haven't signed any release papers, I haven't given my advised consent. I didn't even ask to be here, and I certainly didn't ask for any treatments." Teuton was getting increasingly belligerent.

"You are funny, Mr. Teuton. You asked to know truth. You made that request with great urgency and fervor. When you finish this lifetime, you will look back and see everything happened in its right order and right time for you. Now we will clear you of toxic stuff stored your body. Have some water. Drink lots of it," the woman counseled.

Teuton felt just fine. He guzzled the water and noticed it tasted like the coconut shell he was drinking from. *She probably has a point,* he thought. *I've been around a lot of toxic stuff. Following the safety directions is for weak people. I might have a few toxic chemicals in my body.*

"Come into the sea. You are smelling bad. We'll wash off your skin. Remove your pants; you don't need them, and they will be washed so you can wear them when your body is clean."

Teuton didn't like this a bit. He began to resist; his efforts were clumsy and weak. He tried to speak, but his tongue couldn't form the sounds. He felt out of balance. *I'm drugged. I'm helpless. I need help. I can't call for help. She's taking my clothes off. I can't find my clothes.*

The woman pulled Teuton to his feet. She took his arm and pulled it over her shoulder as she put her arm around his waist to steady him for walking. He decided to cooperate. He found he was able to walk with some coordination and strength. Cooperation definitely improved how well his body was acting. *Man, if I'm not on target here, I can't see well, I can't even move my body well. It's like I have no choice but to go along. This isn't freedom.* His thoughts rambled.

"You don't have freedom," the woman said. "You have toxins. Toxins take away your freedom. We'll make you more free tonight." They began to enter the water.

As the night unfolded, Teuton became quite sick. When he tried to hold back purging, it was worse. He found that he felt better right after getting rid of a batch of toxins and then could easily gulp the water. He got the idea water was needed to dissolve away the toxins and carry them outside his body. The woman was good to her word, always there with him, always taking care of him. He seldom thought about being naked. For the first time he could remember, his nakedness wasn't about sex.

It was as if he were on a lousy drunk he couldn't sober up from. His utterances were whatever was there, demons tormented him, the demons from within. All he could do was be watchful of what was going on for him. He may remember a moment past or not, but if he got lost in his thoughts being him, he got sicker. When he realized and immediately returned to the state of watching, he was still sick, but it was more tolerable.

When Teuton awakened, he noticed the ceiling above him was made of woven leaves. He looked around to see the walls were of bamboo and woven grasses. There was a cool breeze, a sea breeze, pleasant and warm. He saw a saline drip bag hanging on the wall and started a little when he noticed the drip was going to his arm. He couldn't remember feeling so fresh and alive. His whole being sparkled with the freshness of a flowing spring, cascading from a mountainside. He drifted off to sleep again.

When he awoke, the scene was the same except the saline drip was gone and there was a gauze bandage taped to his arm. He looked across the room to see a table with all his clothing on it. Next to the table was a chair with a pair of shorts, a tee shirt, underwear, and thatched sandals on the floor underneath. Teuton felt exceptionally well. He sat at the edge of the bed and then shifted his weight on the floor. He felt fine. So he walked over to the table and inspected his clothing. The thermal underwear bottoms that were removed on the beach were clean. His snow boots, insulated bib-overalls, and parka were folded neatly. He didn't see his gloves, so he picked up the parka. The gloves were found. Everything was there.

This became Teuton's moment of decision. He thought of Dorothy in *The Wizard of Oz* and had ideas of how he might go home. No one was immediately around as he scanned the area, looking carefully for surveillance cameras. He picked up his underwear, put them on, and then proceeded to put on his flannel shirt and pants. Just a few more items, and he would be ready to return to the woods he was taken from, if indeed Sequoia was good for her word.

But this place does not inform or get consent, his thoughts continued. *This place is secretive. It doesn't honor my rights. And who was that kid who drugged me? That was hell! The old man left me on those rocks, knowing I didn't know where I was or how to get anywhere. I don't want anyone using magic on me, like how they took me away from my life.*

Teuton busily put on the remainder of his winter wear. Now he stood like an Eskimo in the tropics. He felt a sense of power and took a moment to revel in it.

"So this is your choice?" He heard Sequoia's voice behind him and swung around to look at her somber expression. Just seeing her activated a ping of something in his heart, yet he felt annoyed with her. *So she's the head jailer, my captor,* he thought.

"You are not captive to this place but to the life on the other side of the portal," she replied aloud. "You cannot have freedom until you have freedom from yourself. I want you to exercise choice. You may choose to return right now. You may return after I have informed you about the competencies we activate for you here. You may choose to develop more competencies, and certainly you will go even if you want to stay. Are we agreed on these terms?"

"Do you have a brochure I can take with me?" Teuton asked.

"We don't operate on that level. We're not a resort. We're not a treatment center. We prepare people in an exclusive, unique program. You are chosen, but I cannot tell you for what you are chosen. You can have a brief tour, and the competencies will be explained to you. Then you can make an informed decision. Normally, we don't use language to communicate these things, but your telepathy is still underdeveloped. I do want to congratulate you on using your 'here-and-now knowing' to get back from the rocks after sunset. That showed you have the right stuff. There's just so much dissonance in you.

"Do you want to return to your life immediately?" Sequoia asked.

Teuton shuffled his weight to his other foot. The heat was unbearable in his winter wear. He began to pull apart the Velcro that held his parka closed over the zipper. Then he zipped it down, took it off, and slung it across the table. Sequoia stood with her hands on her hips as he shuffled his way out of the rest of his gear.

"Now put on the attire on the chair," Sequoia almost demanded of him.

He didn't answer her, yet his answer was in his actions. She continued to be displeased with his attitude. "Yes, you'll have to remove all your clothing to put them on. I'll close my eyes."

Irritation fed his defiance, and he felt his cheeks getting hot. He gritted his teeth as he pulled the thermal top over his head, pulled his thermal pants down to his calves and stepped out of them, and then turned to see if she had really closed her eyes. Her eyes were closed, so he put on the new clothes.

Dennis N. Clegg, PhD

After a minute, he said, "You can open your eyes." But what was even more amazing to Teuton was how his feelings changed in these new clothes. He felt bright and secure. He realized he'd spoken to Sequoia in a pleasant tone. He himself was surprised, whether she noticed or not.

"The first competency is releasing energy patterns stored within you that are triggered by what is familiar in your life," she said. "Think about how you felt when you put on your clothing from back in your life and how you felt when you put on this clothing: fresh, new, and without any associated energy they could trigger."

"Okay, I do feel different. I feel lighter, not because of the weight difference in the clothes. I can feel the changes from the cleansing too. Will I have to go through that again?"

"Not in that same way. In other ways, yes, but it depends upon how attached you are to the stuff you need to release to develop each competency. For instance, you did well with showing you can be in 'action from inaction,' which got you off the rocks. That is one of our competencies.

"If you are ready to go on the tour, I will have Gaia, my administrative assistant, lead your tour while I attend to other matters."

Sequoia turned and departed.

Teuton again listened to his thoughts: *This woman is too powerful. It's no wonder she's in charge. I like women who know how to respect a man and follow him. I don't like her.* Just as Gaia stepped in front of him to speak to him, he cringed. His thoughts caused her to hesitate.

Teuton was not aware of the telepathy communication within C-Know. Unpracticed with telepathy himself, he didn't realize he was still being received, even though he hadn't developed sensitivity for receiving.

She cleared her throat and said simply, "Come with me." She dispensed with greeting Teuton as women were accustomed to greeting men, not displaying her feminine qualities. She wasn't about to play into beliefs she'd heard in his thoughts about Sequoia. Sequoia wasn't the originator or cause of his thoughts, and Gaia would be watching to see what other sexist ideas might go on telepathic display with Teuton.

He hadn't made a good first impression with Gaia. Much as her name implied, Gaia was an earthy woman, well connected with nature. She could have been an Amazon of a matriarchal tribe. She was at least three inches taller than Teuton, with a slender yet strong body. She shone with inner radiance much like Sequoia, and her features would cause most men to stare.

Teuton cluttered up his first impression of Gaia by failing to clear his head of his thoughts as she first appeared. He failed to meet her fresh and new, learning from what she would present of herself for him to notice. He disadvantaged himself with Gaia, something that he would always be putting an effort into repairing.

Teuton followed her to a trail, which seemed familiar to him. As they walked through the vegetation, she said to him, "I understand you want to know truth. But you cannot know truth while holding so much that isn't truth. Your non-truth stops you from learning truth because you judge new information by whether it agrees with the non-truth you're holding." They came to the beach. The tide was out. It was very impressive, the black sand stretching a quarter mile to the water. "You will do much work here getting rid of what you're holding on to. You will become an empty vessel so you can know truth and never again hold onto anything you only think is truth. You spent the night on this clearing beach recently. You cleared a lot of shit! It is good the sand here is black."

Teuton seemed to sink a few extra inches into the sand. *Empty vessel,* he thought. *All my hang-ups, all my conditioning. All the abuse I got as a kid. The religion. Now that's a mountain of beliefs called truth. That's what I thought I would get when I asked for truth. Now they're telling me to become empty? Nice idea. Impossible! But it might be just what I need. Nothing else has worked much.*

"Okay, clearing must be a competency," Teuton said, hoping to redeem himself from the attitude he noticed he was getting from Gaia.

"You're right," Gaia said. "Now we will walk around the island. We will walk on firm wet sand. It is too hard to walk on dry sand."

After about ten minutes of walking in silence, Gaia stopped and removed what little clothing she had on. She was so matter-of-fact; Teuton gulped hard, realizing he was going through a whole lot of stuff

29

coming up he didn't want anyone to know. *She's got a beautiful body. I want to have sex with her,* he thought automatically. There were other people ahead, also without clothing.

"Take off your clothes," Gaia said. "We're going to enjoy the fun in the middle of these people. You'll get over yourself or you won't have any fun. Choice is your freedom."

Then they walked into the middle of about forty nude people, playing like unsupervised children on the beach. A man in the water up to his waist waved and called to Gaia. She ran into the water, splashing wildly as she jumped into his arms and wrapped her legs around him. They hugged and danced and swirled around in innocent delight. Then one of the other men came over and tapped the shoulder of the first man, like a dancer cutting in. Gaia immediately turned and climb into the arms of the second man. She leaned back as he supported her, and they spun around in the water, playing and making noises of pleasure and delight. Teuton looked around to see other men and women gathering to play together in sex play. A woman approached Teuton. "You're new here. Let me show you how to play. I want to be first to make love with you. Are you game?"

Teuton realized he couldn't hide what his body was feeling about what was going on around him.

"Come in with me," she said. "Let's dance!"

He took her hand and ran with her into the water. She wrapped her arms around his neck and jumped up, wrapping her legs around him. She had long dark hair and beautifully dark skin. Her features were made even prettier by soft warm eyes and a beaming smile.

Teuton found it wasn't so easy to be natural and free, but this certainly was a dream come true. He was loaded with thoughts resonating from his conditioning and programming. He felt himself freezing up, feeling guilty and loaded with shame. Either the others didn't see it in him or didn't care. Gaia was nearby; seeing Teuton join in, she danced happily over, tapped the shoulder of his playmate, and said, "I get a turn. The boss will be happy to learn how I played with him." Then she took the other woman's place, who right away looked for another partner.

Teuton reasoned with himself that he would feel guilty later, for these people surely knew how to heal guilt and shame. He was soon exhausted and declined the next woman who invited him to play. He made his way up the beach to the sitting place and plopped down on the ground. Soon Gaia joined him.

"When you are free of fear, and heal all that guilt and shame, you can play all time you want," she instructed. "Fear, guilt, shame all take away your energy. We are building energy naturally and beautifully as we raise our sexual consciousness. Now that you've visited this beach, you will be confronted by your inner robbers. Your robbers steal natural spontaneous energy when you try to live as you were created. An empty container is completely open to receiving."

Teuton was getting the idea. He really would enjoy life more, free of his baggage.

After resting awhile, Teuton began looking lustfully at the women's bare features.

"We're going to the next beach now. You're thinking a mess of confused sexual stuff. You're feeling guilt, shame; doing self-recrimination while wanting sex but so inhibited you can't let go and play. That's a big turn-off here. No one wants to play with a partner all bound up in their heads about sex. All things in the right order and right timing," Gaia proclaimed as she tugged at Teuton's hair, pulling him to his feet. "Glad you were in your body and not your mind when you played with me. The first time is a surprise. After that, the programming in the mind finds ways to get back in control and messes you up.

"You can come this beach when your desire for sex is healthy."

Aw, shit, Teuton heard in his thoughts. *I'm always left out of the fun because of some reason or another. I wonder how long it will take me to not think about sex. That's impossible!* He gathered his clothes and reluctantly followed Gaia, still feeling weak but happy he'd had this experience.

As Teuton walked, his thoughts were all about memories of what happened. He felt tantalized just remembering, and he was following a new lover so he was constantly being reminded. He didn't see much of the area he was traveling through. He hardly noticed whether they were walking through vegetation, sand, or rocks. He didn't notice the tide coming in. If he looked at the world around him, in his thoughts and memories, he could barely see at all. They seemed to walk forever.

Gaia stopped and turned to Teuton. "You keep thinking in the past. You're using your thinking to keep sexual stimulation going in you. We can never arrive at the next beach. Be now. There's no need to think. Just observe. You have not noticed how many times we circled the island. You cannot see the present staying in in past and future thinking. We're traveling in now, but you are not conscious of now. If you don't come and stay in now, we'll be sleeping on a beach hungry. Sex is our amazing birthright. We have sex freely in our bodies, in freedom from our minds. Why keep thinking about sex? Think about the sexuality you are experiencing when it is time for sex and think of other things when it is time for other things. Be fully sexual when it is time for sex. Be fully now whatever time it is. Be present all the time, sexual time and other than sexual time. Be the same each moment, be total to what is unfolding in the moment.

"My legs are tired. We're sitting right here. You find your awareness of the present. See where we are."

They sat for a long time. Teuton noticed he was tired and hungry. He hadn't eaten since the fruit, but he had a lot of energy after replacing toxins with the minerals and supplements his body desperately needed. He was noticing his body, how he was feeling, and began to notice the grains of sand attached to his feet and legs. He looked around and noticed the vegetation; little hoppy crawly critters were moving about. He noticed how happy he was beginning to feel as he saw the world around him. He looked to the beach, very short now, with late afternoon waves crashing and running farther up the shoreline. The water was pretty and fascinating to him. He was intent on the waves, how they ebbed and flowed, like his life. As much as he struggled to maintain himself at some desired point, he would fall back into old habits and express what he didn't want the world to see of him. Then he recovered from thoughts to noticing the moment. He thought how the ocean flowed and ebbed; no one was trying to hold the waves up on the sand. He wondered if he could drop the struggle to be artificially the same all the time, a personality.

"Okay, we've arrived," Gaia announced. "This beach is removing the 'un' part of unconscious. When you experience what is as is, there is nothing hidden to cause trouble. This my favorite beach. Soon your tour will be complete. We just have to walk a little further. Keep consciousness of the moment. Keep noticing now.

"Now look at this beach. People are dancing. The sand stays smooth. No footprints!"

Teuton was spellbound. Indeed, he saw many people dancing harmoniously. He searched the sands after their steps, but the beach was smooth. He had to walk out among the dancers. So he left Gaia and ran to the beach. He felt his feet in the sand as usual, and behind himself were footprints. The people weren't noticing him, so he ran back to Gaia to ask why he was leaving footprints but the dancers did not.

"You don't know Oneness," she said. "You can't celebrate knowing Oneness. You disturb the sand. You are not ready for this beach. The boss wants me to take you to the last beach. You cannot walk on this beach; you can only look from a safe distance away. When I say stop, honor me, and go no further. I protect you, not the beach. Your mind will make crazy things happen."

"But you told me we circled the island," Teuton exclaimed, thinking he'd caught her in an inconsistency. "Then we walked this beach; nothing happened,"

"You definitely were not conscious when we were walking around the island. You were stimulating yourself with thoughts of left-over sex. You do not know whether we walked this beach or not, do you?"

Teuton couldn't argue with her. He knew he didn't know. He'd never heard of left-over sex, but it occurred to him almost all of his sexual life was left over from something that happened, repeating old fantasies. It wasn't an appealing thought.

"What beach is this?" he asked.

"This beach is the unmanifest. Every possibility is there. It is the creation beach. Here energy is an eager accomplice with clear intent. It is a mischievous place with mixed messages and unconsciousness. This is the most secret, protected beach. You definitely are not ready.

Everyone will know from the mess made from your mind. Left-over sex mind will get you in too much trouble.

"Now we go to the evening eating celebration. You make your choice of whether to wear heavy clothes or light clothes. The boss will find you to hear your decision. I will tell her you're not ready. Go home. Practice meditation. Someone else will do your job. The boss is dreaming if she thinks you are right to be here. Maybe her shadow says you are okay. I love her when she's wrong also." Gaia turned to lead the way to the evening meal.

Teuton was trying to formulate who Sequoia was in his mind, seeing her as taking a risk for him, against the better judgment of even himself. Why would she believe in him? It seemed paradoxical to Teuton how she could believe in him while his encounters with her were not pleasant.

The meal was buffet style. The people sat around tables with umbrellas in the center and curved benches. The eating area was of natural grasses, not mowed but kept down from frequent foot traffic. After Gaia left, Teuton helped himself and then went to an empty table. He was playing it safe, observing the people, some of whom he recognized from playing on the beach. His cheeks flushed as he spotted a few women he'd been with, not knowing anything at all about them. He felt torn between continuing with enjoying his sexual thoughts and losing his ability to see the world around him. He moved his focus to being intent upon noticing and seeing things in the present moment. A bead of sweat rolled down from his temple. He thought how curious this dilemma was: suppressing his sexual thoughts and freely enjoying sex. Would he enjoy sex as much if he didn't think about it a lot? The thought brought the fear that sex might disappear if he didn't keep thinking of it. Did he really understand what was going on?

He knew Sequoia may arrive before he made up his mind about what to do. He complied a mental list of pros and cons. He was tormented by guilt and shame for going along so wildly in sex earlier in the day, taking his attention, which only fed the sexual thinking. So he immediately paid attention to what was new around him. It was a repeating cycle. He found himself in sexual thinking, and the awareness instantly became awareness of the moment. He couldn't find clarity with his list, for it didn't seem right in the moment.

There was something about Gaia's attitude that challenged Teuton to prove her wrong. After all, she'd made him feel uncomfortable about his private sexual thoughts that weren't private with her at all. Yet she was his lover. He was getting nowhere with making up his mind. As he suspected, Sequoia arrived before he was finished.

"Make your commitment right now," she demanded. "What does your gut tell you?"

He was stunned. He hadn't seen her approaching. His decision process froze. His gut seemed to reverberate up into his throat and out his mouth with a "Yes." He was surprised.

"Yes what?" Sequoia asked, keeping it up.

"I want to stay here."

"Stay here and be part of the most amazing opportunity you've ever had?"

"Yes, that," he muttered.

"Jump, you idiot! Be total. You sound like you're resigned to go along with something."

Sequoia's voice grew louder.

"Is this how you go through life, going along, never taking the leap or being total? No one here is less than total. This is no place for hesitation. You must want it enough to totally give yourself, to give up who you think you are to find who is under the mess you appear as; if you want all you can have of life, where is the resignation into that weak, silly-ass yes coming from? That's not enough yes for me. I want the yes you're willing to die for. And you will do exactly that here. You'll die as a caterpillar and emerge as a butterfly. I want to hear you're willing to die with the hope of becoming a butterfly, even if something goes wrong and you don't become a butterfly. The only guarantee is you will die as you are. Will you say yes to your death?"

Teuton had never been so intimidated by a woman. His thoughts raced, with adrenaline fueling them. *Am I really that weak?* he thought. *Why is she so hard on me? I thought she was on my side. How am I going to survive this bitch? If I say no, what will she do?* He felt small and inadequate. *Fuck my list. I can't remember it anyway. Is this what I didn't get at boot camp? Bet the guys didn't even see a woman in boot camp. Who ever heard of a boot camp with everybody passing each other around for a quickie, like this place? Nobody would ever believe this! What is my life about? How many suicidal thoughts have I had? Can the bitch read my mind?*

"Yes," Sequoia said out loud.

"No!" he shouted back at her. "No, no, no, no, no! I can't stand my life as it is. No, I can't think of continuing the way I have been going. No to everything I think is important at home. No to my religion. No to my family. No to being afraid to live. No to avoiding taking a stand for myself. Yes, yes, yes, yes, I want to develop all the competencies. Yes, I want to stay here and die as who I am. Yes, I accept the challenge to all I can be. Yes, you've got to give all you've got with the most difficult asshole who ever walked your island. Yes, I will trust you, Sequoia."

He could hardly believe what he heard his own voice saying. Somewhere in him was what earnestly asked to know the truth, and it had taken over.

He looked around and saw that everyone had been listening. They all knew his commitment. He realized he was sweaty and shaking. All his thrill seeking was about wanting to die. It wasn't brave at all. He'd just made the bravest, most daring declaration of his life, and with plenty of witnesses.

"Please show Teuton to his living quarters," Sequoia said to the group, as she turned and briskly walked away.

He soon found himself at the head of a parade, with two people holding his hands and leading him toward a large round building built of bamboo and palm leaves. They approached the building and took him around its outer wall to the left to the entrance; there was no door. He became aware the others were jubilant with celebration. He was led inside; it was dimly lit. He couldn't see any room dividers; lots of mats were stacked at the side of the room with pillows. *This has to be a joke,* he thought. *This is the group room.*

"Here are your living quarters." Gaia's voice surprised Teuton. "You will sleep with everybody. Your business is everyone's business.

Everyone's business is your business. You'll sleep with everyone but are limited to a one-night cuddle with anyone until you've cuddled with all of the women. Now is the time to be thinking about sex. The time for sex is now. Don't mess up your sexual opportunities thinking about something else!"

Teuton was immediately surrounded by women wanting to introduce him to intimacy, comfort, and pleasures. Inwardly, he felt crazier than he'd ever felt, but he knew whatever this was about, he made a full commitment to it. He felt so crazy, he needed freedom from himself badly. He felt himself being touched, and pleasure coursed through his being. He felt desire in the basement prison of his being, pleading to be freed. He quit thinking and let his body express like never before. He didn't think about what he was doing. He was safe here. After all, this place wasn't the same; it didn't operate by the same ideas. He just disintegrated the basement and the prison and became a whole sexual being into the night.

Teuton awoke to loud music and joyful shouting; people were dancing all around. He felt groggy and unable to join in, but he soon found himself being lifted to his feet, as naked as everyone else. As he found balance on his feet, those who had lifted him started moving his body to get him dancing. He'd made a total commitment to this. He found some energy to move. Soon he was dancing wildly, whooping and hollering the celebration of a new day. Then the music stopped, and a voice said loudly, "All men lay in circle."

Teuton took a place in the circle the other men were making. He lay face up, like them.

"Now, ladies sit on a man."

Two women rushed over to him, but one jumped across his torso and claimed him first.

"Now men sit up and hold the lady in the lotus position. Look deeply into the eyes of your partner. Be totally present with your partner. Start this day being totally loving."

Teuton began to understand that if sex was so frequently and freely joined in, he might be able to quit thinking about it so much. *This might just work!*

He was standing in the middle of the grassy area where he'd met his helpers, soon after arriving. Three coaches led him there from the group house. One of the men took charge.

"Now the most basic skill you must master is being invisible." The three walked away, and Teuton couldn't see them anymore. Then he felt a push on his back. "We're here, we were always here. Why didn't you see us?"

Teuton had heard of Australian aboriginals walking away and becoming invisible to those around them. He'd actually experimented with this on the freeway, intending to be invisible to cops. He liked to drive over the speed limit but didn't want to get a ticket for speeding.

"We know you can be invisible sometimes. Save your thoughts and pay attention.

"Did you see any of us in the past months you were here?"

Teuton looked around. The three weren't there. He felt a push on his back again.

"You were in your own thoughts and quit seeing us. You disappeared us. We only gave you a shock by telling you wrong information about how long you were here to put you into your thinking. You did the rest. We simply walked behind you."

"So if I'm in my thoughts, I'm not able to see?" Teuton asked.

"Almost. You also went along with our intention that you wouldn't see. I created two things in your mind: one to occupy your conscious thoughts and one to tell your unconscious mind what to do.

"People don't really see each other most of the time. This is used to our favor. We only make them more blind for our needs.

"This island is invisible; you can make large and expensive items invisible. You will be invisible. It is possible to fool electronics. Nothing will cease to be, but energy fields create an illusion so what is really there is not seen. That is advanced, but you will soon learn advanced methods.

"First change your energy to a frequency we won't see."

After standing there thinking about it, Teuton said, "I can't."

"You're trying to solve the problem by thinking about it. Your thoughts are in language. That is not now, it is thinking about now in language. If you're not in now, you cannot be in choice, in power. Most people are not in now, so they miss what is now. There is no language in now. Go to now ... only now ... and the problem will be answered."

Teuton turned and walked away, and then walked around the circumference of the area to behind the three; he walked forward and shouted, "Boo!" at them.

"When you give up on knowing the answer and let the answer be, there it is.

"We gave you the intention, and in the moment, you found the answer. Now you give yourself the intention."

Teuton turned, walked to the perimeter of the area, and walked right back to be in front of the three. "Boo," he said in a normal voice.

"You tricked us. We expected you to come behind us. You had the additional benefit of us expecting something else. When we expect something else, we don't see what is there. You can create this in people.

"This exercise has permission. Out among unconscious people, some may be trying to be alert and conscious to see you and what you're transporting. They can be helped by their helpers. Psychics and intuitives can be searching. They can't find if they don't know what they're searching for; dowsers can only search for what they know."

Then the three walked straight at Teuton and disappeared.

Teuton stood for a while, wondering if the three instructors would appear again. He tried noticing all he could with his senses. He looked about to see what might be visible, but because he was giving his attention to his thoughts (or some other part of the moment), he hadn't been seeing. He realized visibility and invisibility were happening all the time, and his life had been lived somewhere in the muddled middle. He thought how he was neither visible nor invisible to his world, and at the same time, things weren't clearly visible or invisible to him. He began to be curious about why he'd never considered the subject of visibility before. Suddenly, it wasn't entertainment, like in a sci-fi movie, but a big, overlooked part of life.

He felt impressions and started moving his body. He let go of thinking to see if following impressions would lead his body to know where to go and what to do. He soon found himself walking past his living quarters, down a slight incline to another building that looked quite like his living quarters. He walked around this one to the doorway and went inside. Two people were standing next to a laptop computer connected to a projector. There was a screen, and all of the chairs were facing the screen. There was one chair still vacant. He walked to the chair and sat.

At that moment, one of the instructors began to speak; a woman of African descent said, "For those of you who don't know me, my name is Scera. This is Redbird," she said, pointing to her co-presenter. "He's a Native American."

Redbird turned on the projector and said, "We've got a big challenge you all must become proficient with. To create separation from Oneness is unnatural; I regret to tell you, you'll be developing skills to be aware of Oneness and consciously protect yourselves and what we're up to as a group, by creating separation. You're becoming experts at working with the illusion of separation, maintaining awareness of how our Oneness affects what you're doing."

Changing the slide, Scera said, "This place could be called a Zen commune with a modern twist." On the screen was a picture of the island from the air. "Some of you will choose to participate in a worldwide project. What you're learning today is essential for this island, what we're doing, and the project that is in the conceptual stage of creation. Each of you are recent arrivals. You've been unaware of each other, having your own welcome experiences. You've also had to pass an introduction to invisibility."

The screen changed to a picture of the globe, featuring the Indian Ocean at the center. "We can block electronic surveillance, we can be invisible to passersby. We can even distort light to be invisible to satellite photography. Google Earth sees just the ocean where we are. We can even cause people not to notice there was once an island in the pictures. We can do a lot."

The screen changed again.

"We want to sharpen and focus your awareness so you will not be broadcast stations, each and every one of you as individuals, and that what you're working with is available as little as possible to those searching. We think they don't know what to search for, but if they begin to get the idea of what is possible and scan for it, things will be more difficult.

"First of all," Redbird continued, "you were transported here because part of you was in exact synch and harmony with us in such a way that energies transported us together. Time has actually has no relevance to where you are when you return. It will be exactly one nanosecond after you came here. It was also a strong energetic action that for a brief moment was detectable, should someone have been scanning random energy impulses for patterns. Fortunately, there are an infinite number going on every moment, but few so strong.

"Everyone take a brief break to drink a coconut and take care of your bodily needs. Practice living by your impressions."

When they reconvened, Redbird said, "Okay, everyone. Well done. The harmony of all of you following impressions instead of being told what to do makes a very strong field of group energy. Please bring yourselves back into awareness of this energy when you realize you're in thoughts.

"Close your eyes and think about your daily life. Think about when you don't want people to know the truth about you. Think about the masks you wear, the personality you use like a tool so you get what you want from others. Now think of your frustration and anger when you discover someone lied to you or pretended to be something to get something from you." He paused and then concluded, "You can open your eyes now."

Changing the screen, Scera said, "When we don't give or receive accurate information, we create problems. It is like giving nothing, nothing real, hoping to get something real. But we usually get something we don't like." She changed the screen. "We get the other person's fake information. You are both invisible. I ask you, how can anything real come from that which is not real?"

Redbird began to speak as he changed the screen. "It is like a car that can float like a boat. The wheels splash in the water, and it may work a little, but it needs land, it needs authentic and real ground, because it is a car. It works best on land. Giving the car water it cannot work with instead of a road is what giving inaccurate information is, whether in words or appearance. Everyone is trying to work in invisibility without something they can really go with.

"To become visible and live life with essence and power, every effort must be made to be genuine and give the best information you have available to you, ready to make corrections as you learn more." The screen changed. "Here you are removing the false that society has put into you, that you've learned, so you can know your authenticity." The screen changed again. "With the false removed, you will know who you are. No one is qualified to tell you. You discover yourself."

Scera took the microphone. "Each of you, choose a mask from the table. Put on the mask, and one at a time meet each other and say something to the other you want them to believe about you."

After the exercise, she said, "Stand still for a minute. Feel how it is for you to have someone wearing a mask telling you about them. Do you believe them? Did you say what you wanted them to believe?

"Now drop your masks. Again meet each person. Look into their eyes for fifteen seconds. Tell them something you don't want anyone to know about you."

After everyone had done this, she said, "Now close your eyes and go within. How did it feel to tell about yourself this time? Do you have a sense of freedom? As others told you about themselves, did you feel more trust? Is your heart more alive? Does it want to tell the others you love and accept them just as they are?"

Teuton was aware of himself. He was feeling included and enjoyed how he felt; everyone was more real than they were before. He was surprised what he said about himself and even more surprised how that unburdened him.

Redbird pointed to the new screen and said, "There are many ways we are invisible. In essence, it is because we don't trust ourselves and others. Already in this group, we're building trust. Your lives depend on each other, in every way possible. We will do many things to meet deeply to know and be known as we melt our personalities away and trust meeting each other authentically in each moment. You will not only be visible to each other, you will communicate in thoughts without language and know from each other what you need to know in each moment."

The screen changed as Scera said, "Being invisible is already going on. A camera objectively sees everybody in its view and how they're moving. People don't. Begin to think of your senses as objective. They really are. It is your brain filtering what they sense. If you don't believe something, you don't sense that it is there, even if it is. If you believe that something is a certain way, whatever you are sensing, you will fit it into the way you believe it is, missing how it really is.

"Take the remainder of the day to follow your impressions to wherever they lead you. Notice everything you can. Try to see it as it is. Be yourself without your masks and stories; when you find yourself meeting another person, check in with what you believe about what is there and what cannot be there, then go past your beliefs. Allow whatever is there to be sensed and known, using no language in your thoughts about your experience. Before retiring for the night, we'll meet here again."

Teuton sat there feeling very challenged. It all made sense. It was too simple. Yet he felt inadequate. How could he tell the real truth in every situation? How could he reveal himself? People would surely shriek and run away in horror. And he already knew his vision was limited whenever in his thoughts. He felt inadequate, unable to observe without making words about his observations, not glossing over and really taking time to see. Could he spend a whole lifetime really seeing a square foot of grass? Still, he rose to his feet without thinking about it. It felt right, so he continued to allow movement without thinking but noticing all he could. For a couple of hours, he wandered. He met a couple of men and did some brief and honest sharing with them. His mind was rattling at high speed, or at least he was noticing it more. Each time, he noticed he was briefly back to observing what he could of the moment he was in. Then came the test.

Teuton became aware of a woman in his space. At first, he noticed all he could and sensed all he could about her. He felt changes in his body and began to be fearful. She turned and looked at him. She had a pretty face. She'd been his morning love partner. He was seeing her authenticity, as far as either of them could contribute with only this much practice. Teuton noticed his own authenticity.

"Hi," he said.

That was easy, he thought to himself.

"I love you," she replied.

This caused a chill through Teuton's body, one mixed with fear of all his stored emotional imprints around the phrase "I love you," with his programs about what it meant and what he might do with such a phrase. He wanted to hide, as usual. He started to speak, but words wouldn't come.

How could she be so innocent and matter-of-fact? He thought to himself. He wondered if she was as locked up and terrified as he was.

He started noticing his body. Oh hell, if he were to speak for his body, she'd slap him or report him. His body wanted to have sex with her! He realized how all his life he had to ignore his body and pretend to be something, somewhere else. He usually did really want to have sex with women around him. His body would do outrageous things if his mind weren't in control. He began to rapidly run through all the scenarios he knew of trouble that comes from sexuality, in and out of the bedroom. He felt sick to his stomach. Could he utter his truth?

Seeing Teuton was frozen, unable to relate, she decided to prompt him: "I want to make love with you right now."

Teuton felt his cheeks go red hot and the energy build throughout his body. There could be no denying: his body was clear about wanting to express itself and make love with her. It wanted to move. It wanted him to come home, to be fully in with his body. Teuton felt himself becoming sexual energy, wanting expression.

Looking into her eyes, he gave voice, not to his mind with all its complexities but with the purity of his body: "I want to make love with you right now also."

Then they moved into embracing each other and let their bodies express themselves naturally. Teuton did his best to witness and yet be fully into his experience with her. It was delicious, the most delicious sexual experience he'd ever shared.

They lay, fulfilled, in the grass, holding each other in the afterglow. Teuton had never felt so good, so free, so free of himself. How he loved and appreciated her, so authentic, so real, connected with his very being. He felt her in him, not in a physical way but in his very essence. He could only cuddle with her one night at a time, but he knew he would cherish each night they shared.

After the evening meal signal was given, all the participants joined the community. Teuton noticed each moment all he could and felt; this day, he'd noticed more of the world, more of himself, in just part of one day than in his whole lifetime. There apparently was only one meal a day, with plenty of food available for snacking here, but he didn't seem to need more. He looked forward to noticing the foods, their flavors, their textures, and everything he'd never noticed before. The meal was a completely new eating experience for him, being present to eating.

In the bedtime meeting, Redbird led the group: "As you went through your day, did you notice people who weren't in our group, except at the evening meal?"

Teuton realized he'd only met participants. His beautiful lover sat a few chairs away.

"Others here were invisible to you. It was intended to be that way. They were moving all around you, doing all sorts of things. You were noticing all you could, but they were impossible for you to sense. They noticed you but didn't give any energy to what they noticed. I hope as you met each other, you allowed yourself to give a lot of energy to at least one other participant, going deeply into how it is to merge with another in authenticity."

Teuton smiled and felt a glow as he continued to sense the beautiful woman he'd deeply joined himself with; they had not even exchanged names.

"Tonight, these are your sleeping quarters. Continue to be without words about your experience, but still speak words of genuine truth and authenticity with each other. Don't allow any stories, but just speak to communicate in the moment, whatever is there."

Teuton noticed he was alive with sexual energy. It was real, it was here and now, he could allow it to be felt and noticed; he could speak from his body, not his mind. He realized there was no need for second-hand sexual feelings. Perhaps he was wrong in assuming it was impossible to stop thinking about sex.

The next day, after freshening up, Teuton and the other participants were led to a classroom, where Redbird and Scera were waiting. The group felt an energy, a radiance, an afterglow.

Scera began, "Wow, this group is getting so cohesive! Think of how wonderful you feel right now. Others here have been continuing in this energy. Think of where you were before this group and where you are now. Imagine how it might be when you add to your competencies, like the others have. You will become more involved with those who have been here longer, as your energy comes into harmony.

"Did you notice how many thoughts and feelings came up, that seemed to sabotage your awareness of the moment, living naturally in the moment?"

There was a murmur of general consent.

"Today, we're going to be clearing you of bundles of energy stuck in you for lifetimes and from the generations of your ancestry that are not yours, but that have been affecting you. We're also going to be releasing the bundles of energy that were created by imprints and intensity from your experiences in this lifetime.

"This is the most secret thing we do here. This is what we are preparing you to be: consciously aware of being invisible yet in Oneness as much as possible. You are responsible for protecting all of us with consciousness.

"Actually, none of you can do this right now. You are at a dangerous space for us, putting all of us at risk. However, after undergoing these treatments, you will then be able to do so, and it will speed up and support your expanding competency."

Redbird said, "We've studied ancient methods and modern developments in energy psychology, meditation, Zen, and other approaches. We've used ideas and creations that have come from the beach of unmanifest to combine our personal power in Oneness with electronics to deactivate these bundles of energy that keep giving energy that doesn't belong, that distort your moments.

"You may notice you're afraid to express anger when it is right to express it, because you are overwhelmed by all the energies that come into play. These energy bundles that were created need to be freed and made available for new creations. Then when any expression, anger included, is appropriate in the moment, you can give it all the energy of the moment and nothing else.

"We will not change your memories. Along the way of developing competencies, you will realize that your memories are faulty, that the stories your memories are made of should have expired long ago, and you will finally allow them to end. That you do of your own accord. We won't take away your personal responsibility.

"Today, we simply remove the old energy that complicates the moment."

Scera took her turn: "You will be connected to an invention that shows you flashes of pictures and creates energy patterns that activate old energies. Then energy impulses will target those activated energy bundles and instantly free the energy from you. Energy within you won't exist in that form at all, anymore.

"As it is happening, you may notice feelings and emotions coming, then dissipating, without you doing anything. Just relax."

Redbird said in earnest, "Here is your responsibility: Once you are cleaned of what you have been programmed and conditioned with, you will be innocent, and your abilities will expand to what you may think are super-human levels. It feels that way. Your energies are freed, but you will know only through practice and noticing how you are different.

"The past dies in you and leaves you alive in the present. You will want everyone to have this experience, and the time will come for everyone to have it.

"Take a few moments to think about how interests like companies and governments, religions too, could take this technology and deliberately misuse it or destroy it to keep control of the people. You will be different, so you must practice invisibility. They may get wind of it. The universal consciousness has a lot of chaos with very little clarity, but clarity stands out. You will be clear, living with clarity, and universal consciousness will have your energy in it. If people with certain abilities happen upon this technology we have, they may try to challenge our very lifestyles, wanting to prevent them."

Scera said, "Trust your knowing, and if you find thoughts coming up about this, come back immediately to the moment. Returning will happen automatically. It gets easier as your competency increases.

"We don't ask if there are any questions, and we won't discuss it more than we are in telling you. We avoid putting any energy out that can be detected.

"Please follow us silently, just noticing all you can as we go into the underground laboratory."

CHAPTER 2

———wɯⲟⲟⲉⲧⲟⲟⲧⲉⲟⲟⲱ———

It may have been months, it may have been years. There was no need for
time for people living in the moment, in an energy so palpable it was as if
moving about under water. The only measurements were competencies.
The staff did not test or measure. As the participants developed their
competencies, they would approach the beach of the competency. If
they felt resistance, they would go no further but return to working on
developing the competency. If they could go onto the beach but couldn't
feel relaxed and playful there, they would return to working on their
competency. When finally they could joyously, and in celebration, play
with wild abandon on the beach, they knew they had mastered the
competency. It wasn't the beach itself, but personal responsibility about
the competency and its beach that measured progress.

As people completed their competencies and returned to the lives
they'd left for a nanosecond, Teuton eventually took on the responsibility
to create experiences for new arrivals. He seldom saw Sequoia and
never talked with her again, even once; she was the only woman he
hadn't been sexual with. The rumor was that she was beyond sex, and
the activities of the island operated with her holding a presence for
everyone's experience. Teuton learned that her working with him in the
beginning was exceptional. Some of the staff met with her, but he was
never invited to that level of involvement.

Teuton was so transformed, enjoying his real self, expanding in
himself; he just loved and appreciated being alive. He only felt a little
void, but how important can one little void be when there's so much
abundance in one's self? Sequoia was right about Teuton, and he was

in deep gratitude that she kept him there in the face of the opinions other staff members had about him. He hoped he wasn't coming up on her radar, for he remembered she told him he would return home. He didn't want to return. He was the happiest he'd ever been on the island.

His visits to the beach of the unmanifest were inspiring him with ideas he was working with, and in turn he would go to the beach to manifest creations. He was improving the equipment in the laboratory and adding the ability to remove the subliminal programming the media had been inflicting on the people.

Teuton observed that with the conditioning/programming removed, a person could realize gifts that had been dormant or were unable to be fully expressed for lack of clarity of purpose.

As Teuton worked into his competencies, he found he had energy and passion for helping people to be free of the entanglements that kept them from realizing their unique contributions. He enjoyed seeing them live with clarity and energy, to freely be themselves. As he worked with deconditioning, deprogramming, and neutralizing subliminal messages, he also had a deep sense of responsibility. He realized this: perhaps above all else, C-Know had developed the most important technology to have and to protect. He knew from his own process, removing the soup that steals away people's energy, clarity, and contributions left a void that needed to be filled. If ruthless people and organizations had the technology Teuton was working with, they could create that void in people. Then they would be able to fill the void with whatever served their interests. People would have even less freedom of choice. They could program singular choices so strong that other possibilities would not be considered. Whether to purchase products, or to support political ideologies, or to believe in their constructs of divinity, they could turn people into robots.

Because of this, Teuton knew there must be a safe space and time after dissipating the energy bundles and subliminal programming for each person to develop within themselves a strong sense of who they are, and be certain of their power and choices, before being bombarded by the media and societal messages again. Teuton shuddered at the thought that even C-Know could be tempted to decide what was for people's good; they could become corrupt with good intentions. It was clear to him the system must be protected and watched with diligence, and more than anything else, he and the others trusted to work with developing the machines must remain upright. He studied the assumptions, beliefs, and stories gurus and corporate, religious, and government leaders got lost in. He learned how they would justify taking energy from people, stealing part of their life forces, to exploit it. He must, above all, practice consciousness of doing the work with the single purpose of releasing in each person who they really are, their uniqueness, and the unique contributions they are here to make.

He was absolutely certain, as a steward of the systems of clearing people of the influences that keep them bound up, that there must be no trying to direct, even with justification to prime the pump to get people going, and stay in trust each person will discover and evolve in their own ways and timing.

Could members of C-Know use the equipment to exploit humans? Yes. Unfortunately, yes. But there is a key element of everyone repeatedly going within and making every effort to be conscious of themselves of the people in C-Know that made it a chance worth taking; that gave Teuton the courage to take the risk.

From Sequoia's exploration, her experiences as she sought higher consciousness, she realized that deprogramming and deconditioning people was an ancient practice. She submersed herself in techniques developed in the East to deprogram people from that which prevents them from realizing who they truly are. She collected and studied these techniques, and then she teamed up with geeks of modern technology to quickly and effectively neutralize errors in the human psyche.

Sequoia envisioned the deprogramming system developed by C-Know as an enormously significant development for peace, if used responsibility. She exercised diligence, monitoring and protecting those who worked on its development and refinement.

As Teuton was working, he became aware of a movement he wasn't familiar with. Back when Sequoia first encountered him, he was so unaware he didn't really notice much about her, but something was still familiar. He looked up to see her standing, her energy focused on communicating with him. His heart leapt, even though he was so open and loving with everyone here. His only hope was to listen to her and hope she had business that wasn't going to put him in his old clothing.

For a long time, they looked into each other's eyes. It was different. Teuton noticed impressions without his old energy bundles and noticed many lifetimes of experience with her as his closest companion. No wonder she couldn't be visible while he developed his competencies. This time, the tears flowed in his eyes as he realized the gift she'd given him, the love of her holding space for him while not being in his presence. He knew it would not have gone well had he known too soon what he was now realizing. He couldn't see well enough through his tears to notice tears in her eyes as well. His body took him into an embrace with her, and he felt the familiar heart taken to new levels. They stayed in their embrace as their energies recalibrated to the present. Teuton knew the love he longed to find in every woman all of his life was her, yet under her watch, he found *that* love with everyone here … at least as far as he ever knew loving to be.

Nothing was said as they walked together to her office. Seldom was language used any more for Teuton, as impressions were a more trusted method of communication.

Her bright and elegant office had a desk and an impressive executive chair. Workers had taken special care to weave patterns in the palm leaves and lashings that held the bamboo together. Sequoia spun a guest chair around for Teuton and spun one for herself, facing his. She sat. He took the seat opposite her.

Teuton extended his hands. She met his. They looked into each other's eyes until the energy built so strongly they closed eyes to be with it, within themselves.

When they mutually returned to looking, Sequoia said, "Tell me the mission, your role in the mission."

"I am your partner. It brings me immense joy to join with you again. We are expanding the Center for Knowing Without Knowledge as C-Know, using all that is on this island, gathering anything beneficial for preserving mankind, and equipping seven specially made and equipped jetliners to be guardians of human life. The people who have been here are co-creators with us. When I go home, we will find each other, you and I, and those who have transformed here. We will live a model lifestyle.

"More money than we need will be there as we need it, and we will proceed with everything, knowing that."

"I concur exactly," Sequoia replied. "I will leave the island, and we'll be drawn together again. We will do our work while practicing our competencies in the challenge of the mass unconsciousness.

"One thing I want you to know," she continued. "You may continue with sexual expression as long as it serves you, but I am beyond sexuality. Please understand and respect that it cannot be part of our partnership anymore."

Teuton felt disappointment. He'd become free of all restrictions and repressions of sexuality. Guilt, shame, and fear had no place in his sexual play. Why would the one woman he'd loved from lifetime to lifetime create this boundary? Countless times, they'd made love in many lifetimes. Was the last time in some other lifetime, never to be relived? Could he ever completely feel consummated with Sequoia without continuing as lovers?

He now knew the time was coming to recover from stumbling in the snowstorm in the danger of avalanche at Snowbird. When he returned to Salt Lake Valley and people asked why he was so different, he would simply tell them he had been walking when and where he shouldn't have been one night after an avalanche that wasn't supposed to happen. He would never tell about his island experience.

That night, he spent time with his closest lovers: Alekcia, Ashwini, and Jasmine. He enjoyed the feelings of warmth, closeness, and pleasure, with the sense he wouldn't be enjoying them after that.

The next morning, after again loving with Alekcia, Teuton put his personal space and work space in order. Then he followed his impressions, feeling different from his accustomed island life. He walked past his living quarters, past the eating and celebration area, across the grassy area where he met his team of helpers, and continued on an unfamiliar pathway, eventually arriving at a small clearing, where his neatly folded clothing, the ones he wore when he arrived here, were set on a rock.

His heart sank. He felt sick to his stomach. His body quivered as he felt tears begin to well up. He'd learned to be exactly as he is any moment and to express with the energy of the moment, holding nothing back that would be stored to overwhelm another similar moment. He fell to his knees and wept, expressing his sadness, feeling the same suddenness of shift that brought him here, even though it was unfolding gently this time. He thought of how he might escape this moment to stay on the island. Impressions were, he needed to make this journey to meet again with Sequoia and the others in the other life they'd all taken leave from.

He slowly began to remove his clothes. He didn't look around to see if anyone would see his nakedness. There was no shame or guilt expressing appetites and desires in any moment. He'd come back to his natural self. He knew no need for anything to cover his body, but what would he do about the people seeing him naked in a snowstorm at Snowbird Maintenance Garage? He chuckled at the thought and reached for his thermal underwear.

Soon he was ready. He thought he stood alone. Suddenly, from invisibility, all the people he'd been developing proficiencies with were there. He knew without words, as they did. He took a good look around. He knew he knew and would always know what he needed in the moment, not before, not bothering to ruminate on after. They would all continue together, including those who already returned that nanosecond of moments later.

He joined his mittens in a Namaste position and bowed from his waist.

Teuton recovered from stumbling and stood in the winter scene. Out of habit, he was aware of his impressions. He turned off his flashlight, closed his eyes, and moved each moment as he was impressed to do. There was no thought of fear, only trust in the moment having answers and abilities as expedient.

He noticed the familiar roar of the big T-rex loader, and lights illuminated his eyelids. He knew the big machine was coming to remove the snow of the avalanche from the roadways. He knew the driver might not see him over the huge scoop that led the way, so he climbed up the snowbank that gave definition to the road. Then he giggled, feeling the playfulness of a child as he slid down the snowbank after the T-rex passed.

CHAPTER 3

—ᵕᵕᵒᵒᵉᵗᵒ᷍ᵒᵗᵉᵒᵒᵕᵕ—

Teuton quit his job at Snowbird, took care of his belongings and personal affairs, and prepared to leave the Salt Lake Valley. He sold or donated all the belongings he felt encumbered him, leaving less than a carful of things to take on his next journey. He went to his bank to close out his account. The teller seemed to take forever to conduct the transaction. He felt impatient with the delay. He felt a touch on his left arm and turned to find an immaculately dressed woman who said to him, "Sir, will you please come with me?"

Teuton imagined all kinds of scenarios as he followed her through the building into an elevator and up to an administrative floor. He thought perhaps he'd been garnished. Perhaps the IRS seized his bank account. Perhaps he was overdrawn. She led him to a desk. Two men were standing there on opposite sides of her desk. He realized his thoughts had dropped into the past and were making stories of the future instead of being in moment. That realization brought him back into the moment.

The two men said nothing. The woman looked at her computer and then took a sheet of paper off her desk. Then she addressed him, saying, "Sir, there's an irregularity with your account. The Patriot Act requires an investigation into this kind of thing. You've been a very average wage earner and spender. You've never had a savings. We've got to investigate your account balance."

"There must be some mistake," Teuton replied. "I'm living on my final paycheck. Is that a violation of the Patriot Act?"

"Sir, when there's a sudden jump in an account balance, the government of the United States wants to know why, for their own safety. This isn't a final paycheck Snowbird would give. You're not the company CEO! These men are taking you in for questioning."

Teuton found himself handcuffed, and the men took his arms on either side, led him to an elevator, and walked him to a car in the parking garage. He was blindfolded, his belt was removed from his pants, and he was pushed onto the back seat; the car drove off on a long ride. Nothing was said. The moments seemed odd to Teuton. His impressions remained okay with what was happening and without anything to do, without any information he needed. He just patiently waited and noticed all he could about his blindfolded ride.

He became aware the car stopped and the driver had to identify himself with a guard. There was a gate opening, another closing behind. This could be jail or a prison; his thoughts returned to words. Aware of his thought, he instantly noticed again. He remembered on the island how awareness in the moment kept him clear and ready. The car drove on but too far for a police station parking lot, and there were turns. He began to notice the smell of jet fuel and the sound of jet engines. The car came to a stop. Teuton's thoughts fell to wondering how his bank account could warrant such extreme measures.

What kind of monster is the Patriot Act anyway? He heard in his thoughts.

The men exited both sides of the car. The back door opened, and Teuton felt a hand around his arm that began pulling him. Still, nothing was said. Once his feet were out of the car and he found balance, the other man took his right arm, and they began moving him toward something. He felt something bump his shin, and his instinct was to step up. It was a step. He sensed he was going up the steps of a bigger airplane than he flew, possibly a corporate jet. At the top step, the men stopped his motion. The handcuffs were unlocked. Teuton sensed the moment. No impressions to do anything except go along. Hands pushed on his back and others pushed his head down. He must be entering an airplane with a door not big enough to pass through standing fully upright. He stepped inside. Then he noticed the hands had stopped directing him. He waited for what would be next. The door closed and was latched. He didn't sense the men inside the plane with him, so he reached up and removed the blindfold.

The plane was luxurious. This couldn't be taking him for questioning. He looked around at the seats and tables. It wasn't a large plane but big enough to offer comfort and some amenities. He reached for the back of the seat nearest him and moved into it. He was shaken and took a moment to sit and regain his composure. He was safe in the moment; with some composure, he could get clarity of what to do. He noticed an engine starting. He'd noticed the cockpit was cordoned off from the passenger area. There must be pilots, but why would he be left alone, unrestricted?

The plane began to move. He heard the second engine winding up. They sounded like aft-mounted engines.

"Hey Teuton! Get up here. I need a copilot!" The female voice was familiar, yet the sound system disguised it. He felt bewildered, and as he rose from his seat, he felt his balance was off. *What kind of game is this?* He thought.

He opened the door to see a woman sitting in the left seat, with headphones on. He made his way up the middle to take the vacant right seat. He had to figure out how to get through the narrow passage with controls between the seats. He noticed a headset was placed on the dash. He wiggled into the seat, took a deep breath, and then looked to see who the pilot was. Who he saw so surprised him he sat motionless in awe, aware of the sweat he'd worked up getting into the seat. She was talking on the radio, intent on guiding the plane.

It was Sequoia!

Finally, she looked over, catching his eye. He was a silly sight for her, eyes wide as saucers, mouth agape in a comical pose. So far, he wasn't able to speak. She winked at him and said, "Put the headphones on. I want to talk with you."

Teuton's heart did its usual thing when he'd meet Sequoia. He scrambled for the headset, noticing it was of high quality. He put it on and only uttered, "Hi."

Sequoia mused at her creativity. She'd just pulled off the best caper of her life. She arranged everything and kidnapped Teuton. "We've been cleared for taxi. I'll be busy for a few minutes. I'll explain all of this once we're at 10,000 feet."

Teuton sat, astonished. He listened to her radio work and watched as she skillfully did all the steps of piloting, steering with her feet and making settings on the dash. She was adept with the glass cockpit features, something Teuton had only heard about but had only used once. They held short at the end of the runway and switched to the radio frequency for flight. They were cleared for take-off.

Teuton was surprised how much this plane pushed him into his seat, how fast it accelerated, and how soon the nose lifted. Then he got what he always wanted, a rocket ride upward, laying more than sitting and feeling acceleration. The childlike wonder of this airplane was helping the memory of his ordeal to get here drift further back in the past.

She leveled for a gentle climb and trimmed the plane. She requested westward departure, clearance was given, and they banked left. Already the Salt Lake Valley was disappearing behind him.

"Okay, we can talk now," Sequoia told him.

"Do you always do this—take people without warning?" Teuton asked.

"I'm sorry," she said.

"What happened back there?"

She replied, "I made arrangements with your bank. Telepathically we were in communication, at least I was listening to you, and so I set up the whole thing. My family owns that bank. Those guys work for us. This is my airplane. I guess you don't remember our lifetimes enjoying privilege.

"Anyway, you were being tracked. We needed to be getting on with our work together and needed to create a believable scenario for your disappearance. The bug you didn't see attached to your belt was dropped in a homeless area. And I couldn't wait to see you again."

Teuton's eyes watered upon hearing her affection for him. At that moment, everything was forgiven and appreciated. All he needed of her story was that she couldn't wait to see him. He reflected on the proficiencies and how everyone on the island unabashedly spoke the truth. He looked within to get an idea of what the truth of the moment was he could speak. "You're an idiot. A really good idiot, but an idiot all the same."

They burst into laughter.

"If you don't want something dramatic to bring us together," she said, "stay close."

As they continued to climb to cruising altitude, Teuton silently pondered his inner turmoil about how many "motivators" he'd placed his hope in. He hoped he was doing just what would make a change for himself and the whole planet. He thought of the threats of punishment of the legal system, replacing the threats of punishment used by families, caretakers, and educators to get children to be compliant. He thought how prisons were more a university for criminals to become more expert at crime than places of rehabilitation. He compared all of it with the way he had transformed so much on the island.

He thought of all the predictions he'd heard and was threatened about in his lifetime. He tried to remember all the times he had seen a prediction come and immediately fade away, as everyone on the planet continued without the slightest bump of interference.

"Sequoia," he began, speaking gently, "I admit I feel disappointed. I wanted something to happen to change the way life is, the way we are. That is what the predicted events were supposed to do: change us."

"Well, yes," she replied, "but deadlines are essential to getting work done. Predictions motivate people, give them a reason for persistence."

"Okay, who is creating the lies, then, to get people motivated? Where do the predictions come from? What about all the false alarms, the predictions that haven't happened? That demoralizes people when they've worked toward a deadline and are prepared, only to see nothing happen. People talk about predictions but they don't do anything to prepare after repeated false alarms. False predictions work against real ones."

She replied, "The changes can't come about by a super-punch of more of the same. All that will do is produce mega doses of more imprints of fear, pain, suffering, and misery to carry forward in a humanity just longing for healing.

"We're too imprinted with loss, trauma, shock, suffering, threats that if we don't do what we're told to do, something terrible will happen to us. It's why we're so injured and want a deliverer to heal us. Armageddon was a super-threat of more of that. There were popularly held predictions in Y2K and again in 2012 that were supposed to be Armageddon. It was supposed to produce peace … freedom from the suffering of humanity. Believers somehow bought into the idea the most extreme punishment of all would finally work to produce a healed life for all who survived. How could different results come from intensifying what we need healed from in the first place?"

Teuton reflected as they continued their flight. Perhaps there would be no saviors, there would be no deliverers, there would be no beings in other dimensions, or other frequencies, or any other, other.

"*Mi amiga*, what are you trying to tell me?" Teuton asked.

"Did anyone punish you into developing competencies that transformed your life?" she asked.

"Of course not. What are you getting at?" he replied.

"Your motivations come from your heart in coherence with your mind. You aren't motivated with threats and punishments. You avoid suffering and pain to have as little as possible, but it is love that heals you to be free and expansive. In love you heal the imprints of all the things that hurt. Then you are free of their influence on you."

"So all the doomsday threats … let me reflect on this a bit … are attempts to use fear to manage people? If people can be drawn into fear, they are less aware of love, and it is easier to sell them on the need to be rescued … from the fear stuff? It may get people to be compliant with more threat of adding to the woundedness they already have, but it isn't working." Teuton was beginning to shift his perception.

"No, but love always does," Sequoia said proudly.

"So instead of predictions of a monumental event pushing the buttons of unhealed misery we fear getting more of, we need to turn to love in a monumental way, being the force that goes viral and heals the imprints?"

"Come on, amigo, if everyone on the planet could have one quality that makes your life wonderful, what would it be?" Sequoia kept moving toward her point.

"Love, of course," he replied.

"So let's change the tide here. Let's start going around telling about the imminent, inevitable advent of love expanding in everyone and healing us all. Then we'll tell everyone what comes from their true beings will make this planet the most amazing place ... more amazing than anyone could possibly guess."

As the Sierra Nevada Mountain Range of California's east side was coming into view, Teuton pondered how the cockpit of an airplane was his most relaxing setting, the most in-the-moment place, and how he was thinking about other things, something he wasn't aware he'd ever done before. He reasoned it was because Sequoia was doing the flying.

"I heard there's a place in Scandinavia where seeds from all over the world are stored," he said. "I have had this idea. What if all the worthwhile information about everything useful and of benefit to mankind were to be gathered in one place and kept where no earthquake, no meteor hitting the earth, no war, no catastrophe could stop it from being available to people who survive such things?"

"What would that be?" Sequoia replied. "No place on earth could guarantee such things. We have evidence of mountains having once been the bottom of the sea. The seeds in Scandinavia are of no use if they are buried and inaccessible, ending up in the sea."

"Airplanes could do it," he said excitedly. "Airplanes could be kept in the air through a catastrophic event with seeds, information, tools, and all that. Then they could come back to earth in the aftermath of a catastrophe."

"That is worth looking into. Where do you want to go, amigo?"

"Someplace warm," he said. "How far can we go on our fuel?"

"Let's set down in Sedona, grab a bite to eat, make a flight plan, and top off our fuel." She said as she banked the plane hard left 110 degrees. "We can't go more than 1,500 miles on a fill-up, so we've got to stay in the Americas. There are some pretty exclusive resorts hidden around, and most of the people there will have developed their competencies on the island."

"Take me to your favorite then," he said.

There was silence between Sequoia and Teuton for a time. He was taking in where he was, the airplane they were in, how life was changing from what he had known, and living in a whole new realm of possibilities.

He finally broke the silence: "Sequoia, why the kidnapping and an airplane? Why wasn't it done with a portal again? Why do we need an airplane to go anywhere?"

"Good you noticed. Portals work between dimensions, but they don't seem to exist within one dimension. I'm using my airplane because we're staying in the same dimension, and we can't transport dense material here without machines."

"So, your island was in another dimension?" he asked.

"Not only in another dimension. It was on the planet that has seeded life on this planet several times; our parent planet."

"Okay, so we can transport by a portal to a planet light-years away in an instant, but we can't transport the same way here?" Teuton asked thoughtfully.

"Not exactly. There are parallel dimensions here that coexist. For instance, entities that are not in bodies are all around; most people don't perceive the wavelengths they exist on. They just aren't in bodies. There are times they are perceived, and you've become quite adept at working with unseen helpers. Most people are operating in their limited beliefs, and it is all convoluted for them."

"Okay," he said, "so there are layers of existence here at the same time, and we are so close to our parent planet, we transport through portals in exactly one-half of a nanosecond." Teuton sounded confused.

"Get out of your knowledge and into the moment. Check with your knowing."

"Why didn't you tell me the island was on the Pleiades? Did you lie to me?"

"Truth is in evolution. It never arrives. It is always in expansion. What wasn't revealed to you wasn't non-truth. You were told truth, as you were able to grasp it without total overwhelm. You were on the Pleiadian Island to develop and practice your competencies, not to learn all about interplanetary transport. You were in that aspect of truth, and that was a big stretch for you in the beginning. Now you know there's an island in the ocean, also called the Indian Ocean, on a planet near the Pleiades that we call the Pleiades. The use of the word 'India' didn't start here, just like the Sierra Nevada Mountains of California are named after the Sierra Nevadas of Spain. We do that. The name was used on Arcturus too! They're our grandparents. What is even more interesting, another aspect of truth, is that the island coexists on both planets. Now put that into your mind map."

"So why are we here on this planet?"

"Time for another knowing check, Teuton. You've got to learn to go there first and quit trying to know from your head. You're trying to borrow information instead of owning it."

After a pause, he spoke again, saying, "We're Pleiadian from being seeded thousands of generations ago, and we're in trouble. So our Pleiadian parent planet is helping us, one person at a time."

"Good. You do know. So do our readers! We cannot live in our truth for our communication, because we have to use words instead of telepathy for our readers. Yet between the lines, telepathy is there. Those readers who are experiencing with us sense the telepathy too."

"We're drawing our readers into aspects of truth they haven't been aware of, except for a rare few. Yet in the silence before conceiving of using language about the moment, they're with us! Their knowing is in our story. We're just relevant enough and possible enough to activate their associative knowing." Teuton just let the words drift into his microphone.

"So we're telling more truth through story," she said, "because it is easier to assimilate truth in story form than to be confronted directly with it. We have a messenger witnessing and writing about us. Readers are journeying with us."

"It is in our knowing, and it is in the readers' knowing, when they go into their knowing space. The story we're living is a relevant possibility, but their knowing takes them into further exploration of truth with their own life experiments."

"Oneness is always there, just an awareness away! We're one with each level of the story from living it out, to the witness writing about it, to the readers activating their knowing about it. It is all truth flowing in Oneness."

Sequoia's voice brought closure to the conversation.

They sat in silent communion the remainder of the flight to Sedona.

CHAPTER 4

As they were waiting for the main course of their lunch to be served, Sequoia couldn't help but notice how out of place Teuton's mannerisms were. The Yavapai Restaurant at the upper level of the Enchantment Resort Clubhouse had a large patio overlooking Boynton Canyon's famous formations in the Red Rocks area of Sedona, the same strata as the Grand Canyon National Park to the north. The Southwest décor blended with the stunning views; the area was within the northernmost and largest of Sedona's famous energy vortices.

Sequoia's family owned the casa at the northeastern side of the resort, and it was available for a list of friends and family at the cost of maintenance, amenities, and resort management costs, as were other properties around the world nestled in world-class resorts. Sequoia sat enjoying the views and company with Teuton, drifting in and out of fond memories of time she previously spent at Enchantment.

She noticed Teuton was taken by the experience. He was nervous, looking around and trying to grasp his situation, and his speech lacked confidence. When he looked at the menu, it was obvious it was difficult for him to order. She wondered how he was feeling, being provided for and not paying his way. He had had the J-O-B throughout his life, just as a good working-class citizen was scripted to do. He would have to work for days to pay for a lunch here. The tip would be more than he'd spend on a date at a nice restaurant.

She finally decided to interrupt his space. "Teuton, *mi amigo,* one of the competencies you couldn't develop on the island is living in birthright abundance. You might think I was born into one thing, and you were born into another."

"Well, yeah. It's pretty obvious. I was born poor to ignorant and abusive people who told me repeatedly I would always be poor. I was told to make the least of choices, leaving the better choices for others. I was taught to fear and respect those who were better off than me, which was about everyone. We rarely ate out, and then it was drive-in fast food or a rare greasy spoon restaurant. I was always to order one of the cheapest choices on the menu."

"Amigo, come back," she said gently. "Look at me. Can you go into the moment and know for yourself?"

Teuton took about thirty seconds. He closed his eyes and sat still. "No. I feel overwhelmed and in conflict. This wasn't supposed to happen to me, things like riding in a personal jet and going to an elite resort. That is for other people."

"Very good," Sequoia said, coaching him. "Look into what's going on for you right now. There's no need to come up with any stories or answers. Just know what is there. This is what is going to be your challenge, your transformation. Just notice how it is for you each moment. I'm not going to judge you. Right now, I know you at a level you can't allow yourself to really know. You might talk about it, but you haven't been able to know, because you haven't been in the situations."

"This is really surprising. I dreamed of being wealthy. I thought I knew something about it. You're offering me infinite resources, but if I lose your approval and you decide to stop sharing what you have with me, I'm screwed." Teuton dug deep into his honesty.

"That makes a rift between us, and that's not acceptable to me." She replied, "We can't be in an unequal relationship. Even if we purport to be friends, you'll act more like a placating servant, like a beggar, than as my equal. I can't pretend to be less than I am, for you or anyone else."

At that moment, the food was served, and their attention went to eating.

After eating, Sequoia led him to the front desk, where she checked on the availability of the casa. Teuton looked around, trying to find some comfort with his surroundings. He could feel such pain, such separation from all that was around him. He noticed people moving about with ease and focus on whatever they were doing and felt awkward, standing like a stranger who had just arrived on earth for the first time. He wondered if others were judging him and noticing what a misfit he was … or at least he felt like he was.

Teuton felt chills in his body; he noticed his fingers and feet were cold, and the temperature of the clubhouse was set too low for his comfort. He shifted his weight to the other foot, realizing he was frozen to one place on the floor. He saw a bellman at the entry door. He couldn't even imagine being that close to the rich and famous. He'd been the guy in basements and attics, keeping the equipment working. He was the behind-the-scenes guy, keeping things comfortable for others, who didn't notice he existed. Here, he stood out of place. Would people think he was the servant to the beautiful, poised, and confident Sequoia? After all, he was standing a few feet behind her, unattached and inattentive to whatever she was doing.

The person at the desk went into the back room for a moment. Sequoia immediately noticed what was going on with Teuton. Once again he was in his mind, but at least noticing what was going on. He wasn't pretending to be something he didn't know how to be, if anything really being honest with himself. She could feel it like a rain shower of syrup. She realized she had no idea of how to help him through this moment, let alone whatever else it would take to get him up to speed with being an equal; she longed for him to be equal. She took a moment to notice how she was feeling. She realized she didn't think he was an equal either, and there really was a chasm, her own chasm, equal to his. The love in her heart pained at the realization he not only couldn't be her lover, he couldn't be her equal, and she had her own abyss to deal with about it. No wonder she had to kidnap him, she now realized. She didn't know how to invite him into her world, and he would have had difficulty accepting what she would offer.

The front desk clerk returned. "Ma'am, the casa is already occupied with a party of twelve. I'm not at liberty to tell you who they are."

"Thank you very much," she replied politely and then turned to Teuton.

Their eyes met, but it was an uneasy meeting. There was indeed a void between them, something that was superseding the love they'd remembered looking into each other's eyes on the island. That was new. That was easy. Teuton was in a place of neutrality and didn't know how vastly different their lives were on the other side of the portal. He was a puppy on a leash, following her in her comfort zone, but he was also a man, proud, too proud to surrender to being provided for like a child. That would never work. Her celibacy was no longer the issue between them. It was much more vast than meeting sexually. The moment had an answer, but could the uncomfortable energy between them be left to notice what the answer in the moment was?

"Let's go," she blurted out, motioning for him to come with her toward the entry doors. "Let's get out of here."

They walked silently down to the road at the bottom of the canyon. They came to a bench at the side of the golf course. Teuton stopped. She turned to see what he stopped for, facing him.

"I need to say a few things," he began. "I'm overwhelmed. I don't know how to love you like I know I do, be your platonic friend, and have you completely keep taking control of my life. Excuse me, but you're used to being in control, and you do it well. Don't you think that's a little control-freakish? I mean, you take over my life, you take over my person. Sure, it's beautiful; sure, it's elegant; sure, it's like the dream everyone would want, but you completely take me over! I need to go for a walk. I need some time alone. I've got my own money, a credit card, and I can meet you at the airport terminal at sunset, if you'll allow me that much control of my life."

Sequoia was shocked; she couldn't believe what she was hearing. No one had ever confronted her like that before. She knew he wasn't coming from past stuff. That had been taken care of. This was purely here-and-now energy, built up by what was going on between them. She couldn't accuse him of being out of control with anger. He was being appropriate and letting her know what he was observing, what he wanted, making boundaries, and offering an agreement to come back together, although he didn't say what he wanted her to do, whether to meet him at the air terminal or anything else. She knew she had no alternative but to agree with what he was stating. There was nothing to negotiate.

"Okay, Teuton. I apologize for my insensitivity. I'll meet you at the airport." Her voice was wounded and contrite.

Teuton briskly departed uphill in the canyon. Sequoia knew he would find a gate and a trail that joined the public trail up the canyon, past the ruins and natural beauty. She also knew he might get in trouble, as the shadows of the sun lowering in the west would drop temperatures. She realized she was in caretaking mode with a rugged survivalist, who could probably teach her a great deal.

She turned and walked toward the entry gate.

She made her way up the end of the eastern ridge of the canyon to rock formations visited by hundreds of people a day. She found a private place to sit, where the sun would still warm her, and sat in her accustomed lotus position.

For the first time in her life, Sequoia wanted something perilously out of balance, because she'd pushed it too far, and it might tip utterly away from her; with the very best of outcomes, it might tip back toward her. She imagined a rock like the formations around her, large at the top and with a small base, tipping almost to falling over the ledge it precariously sat on. She realized she'd done what she was accustomed to doing, and it had pushed this rock formation away from her. She pondered how she assumed ownership, how she assumed he would be grateful for all she offered. She offered a lot. Her abundance was endless. To her, it was generosity. Why didn't he gratefully receive it like other people do? It was nothing to her, just something to give. It didn't take anything away from her to give, but was it really giving without control and expectation? The thought hurt. She felt chills down her spine and out her feet.

She was raised to try other possibilities if the ones she wanted at first weren't good choices. No one told her she was wrong, they just redirected her attention to something more acceptable. Actually, she'd committed a crime. She'd kidnapped someone, and did it in such a way it had shocked him. What a way to be controlling! Then she treated it like a favor, a joke. She began to see the rock teetering even further, hearing rock at the base shatter with the strain.

I wanted him near me, she thought, *yet I deceived myself. I justified I was doing what was good for him without him having any input. No wonder he's upset! I tell him I love him while I'm controlling him. What love is that? In my world, everyone is controlling each other in some form or another and, at the same time, loving each other. I didn't earn my money, I didn't have to earn anything ... or did I? Didn't my brother get disowned? Isn't he out in the world, making his own way? Aren't I better at pleasing and getting everything I want in abundance? Aren't we all so secure, having wealth from generations, old money no one for generations even knew how to earn? It's there, I am grateful for it, I use it generously, just like my family does.* She swallowed hard. *Conditionally. I just don't see the strings attached, because I am so good at pleasing the family, pleasing our friends, not pleasing Teuton.* She watched the language of her thoughts speaking.

She became silent, realizing she'd never allowed herself to see this. She knew there was deeper, much deeper, to go within herself. Outward courage, surface bravery pleased people but wasn't going to stop that rock from breaking free and toppling over the ridge. She wanted to be equal with a man; she thought she would raise him to her level, and he'd be so grateful. Except he just confronted her and walked away.

She had to face more of herself, go deeper. Everyone on her island peeled away layer after layer to their very being, while she'd been the authority, owner, and principal of what served them. It was always unequal. Her celibacy declaration kept her unequal, while others grew and developed in loving expansively. Someone was cheated, and the person who cheated her was the one cheated. She'd made her own circle of exclusion.

Deeper she sank into herself as words no longer came, just images. She breathed deeply, let go of her breath, and went deeper yet into herself. To put anything into words would be to exit the moment to create language about it. She just observed whatever morphed back and forth in her inner submersion.

Teuton walked with force. He felt like he'd betrayed a benefactor, like he was pushing away all the goodness a man could want from life. *How can I feel such love for a woman who has not met me, has not negotiated agreements with me, who just does whatever she wants for my good?* He thought. *Do I love being controlled? Do I love the conflict I have to overcome to relate with her like I think it should be? Do I make up past life stories to explain what I shouldn't try to explain? Is this love addiction or do I really love this woman for some unknowable reason worth working through everything, peeling away the layers, to reveal the purity of? If I break this control thing and establish myself as her equal, will I lose all feelings of love and passion for her?* His thoughts were deeply honest and painful all the same.

His feelings were expressed in every movement of his body as he pounded the ground with each step. He was mad but couldn't clarify the soup of his anger. He was mad at his heart, he was mad at his thoughts, he paused on the trail and realized if he didn't communicate with her and close the chasm between them, he might never resolve the power of his feelings in this situation.

He stopped where the trail passed through a clearing. He repeatedly jumped up, fists clenched, and as his feet pounded the earth beneath him, his hands also pounded an imaginary plane, like the ground was for his feet. At that precise moment of slamming downward, he let out a gush of sound. He did this over and over, allowing everything he was feeling to be expressed. Then after only a minute or so, he stood there, limp, breathing hard, exhausted, and sweat causing his clothing to cling uncomfortably to his body.

Just then, some hikers returning down the canyon excused themselves as they walked past him. He didn't care what they saw or what they might think of him; it helped him get clear of what needed to be released. After all, being deceived in a kidnapping stirred a lot of energy he couldn't fight against.

His thoughts began to make sense: *Okay, I've got to go back. I've got to talk with her until our energies meet again. I've got to take my place as an equal partner with her this evening, even if it means she flies off in her pretty jet without me. I don't care how wonderful what she's offering me is, it already feels like a prison. I wonder how it is for her? Is she a prisoner to all the abundance available to her? Is there a prison wall where if she displeases someone, she's cut off from everything? Is she really very poor, absorbed in uber-wealth that's conditional? Is my final paycheck more mine than everything she thinks she has? Is she just a little girl with pretty toys she's told are hers that can be taken from her?*

He went deeper into himself: *Haven't some people recognized something in me, an energy of privilege, of being better than? Haven't I been called "sir" in the tone of royal respect by some close to me? Haven't I been insubordinate, thinking of others as lower than myself? What of my arrogance when people challenge my failure to respect authority, and I tell them the person in authority hasn't earned my respect? Isn't there something of me, an energy of my being that has wealth, power, fame, admiration, and everything that comes with the wealthy, ruling, royalty class in me? Can I see into Sequoia's lifetime? She's right, I have lifetimes there, and it is my nature.*

Teuton's conditioning began playing in his thoughts. Who was he to dare to consider himself more than what was beaten into him of his lowly status among others? Who was he to even think himself in a higher station than those who had bullied him and turned him into a cowering, frightened beggar? Who was he to get higher education and think he could leave the life of his heritage behind him? Who was he in the Enchantment Club House, between the world he was supposed to be in, but which was it he was supposed to be: the conditioning and programming of preparation for this lifetime, or the reconnection with the lifetimes of privilege to go onward with this current lifetime?

Teuton's thought stream went on: *I'm seeing the conflict. I've dragged along the image of myself I was beaten into accepting. I haven't allowed it to change, as I have done all I have to transform myself. I have an idea of what I look like to others, and it is what I was made to look like to myself when I was being jerked up. How humorous; I wasn't raised up, I was jerked around, and it wasn't even up! I hate all they did, and I've disowned it for a better life. The better life is here in unimaginable glory, and I am loyal to the past image of myself I have been dragging behind me. It looks like a sled load of rubbish and slimy, rotten stuff. It has a rope I have slung over my shoulders, as I keep pulling it along with me. It isn't other people seeing my old image. They probably see me as I am, very transformed. I am still pulling the sled of my past images along with me and haven't decided I could just let go of the rope and go on unencumbered.*

As Sequoia went deeper, the solution appeared. On the other side of the balancing rock was Teuton's energy in yin, receptive mode, and the imbalance put the rock in peril. Sequoia was coming from her yang energy out of balance, pushing the rock. She saw the need to bring her yin energy to soften her yang and find her inner balance, allowing Teuton's yang energy to come into balance with his yin. The rock balanced in equal yin and yang energy. The forces of her and him on opposite sides of the rock must find the balance, each on their own, then meet in a flow of balancing within and with each other. Then she saw the rock return to its full upright position, balanced.

She realized she must, absolutely must, be receptive and wait for him to come to her to begin the balancing process, even if he made another choice and she never saw him again. This was her time to wait and nothing else. Self-doubt breathed in her face. Trying to remember waiting without asking, without people scrambling to give her what she wanted, trying to remember a time she didn't go after what she wanted, assuming she would get it because she always did; could she wait, passively, nonaggressively, nonassertively, no reaching out and pulling it to her? *Wait?* She began to realize she'd never been that vulnerable to wait in the void of the unknown, letting others choose her ... or not.

Teuton went down the canyon and marched through Enchantment, instead of using the public trail, and walked with unquestionable authority past the guard at the guardhouse. He was letting his inner knowing take him. He knew he wasn't going to the airport. He was going on another adventure. Maybe he would see Sequoia again, maybe he wouldn't. Maybe he'd never see the Sequoia he'd been perceiving her to be; perhaps he would see a new Sequoia, who would meet him in the different way he now felt about himself.

He made his way to the parking lot for the trailhead. He saw a big mirror on a pickup truck and looked around to see if anyone was watching. He walked to the mirror, moved it to meet him square on, and took a look into the eyes of the transformed man he'd always chased after, with addiction to the chase that never ended. He looked deeply.

He thought to himself, *Who is this person, if I were looking at him and didn't know he is me?* He looked with intent to see. He saw a man wise, a man gentle and powerful at the same time, a man he would spend a long time sitting and learning from, a man he would trust to guide him his whole life. He looked deep into the eyes and realized a deep love merging with the man in the mirror. He saw an average man powerful enough to be whatever he needed to be and strong enough to support others in exploring their own power. He saw a man so powerful he had no need to overpower anyone else. Nothing to prove, he realized his journey had been in circles and it was enough, but he hadn't allowed himself to be enough.

He gently pushed the mirror until it clicked into its usual position. He stood and felt his own presence. He noticed one of the trails served by the parking lot and trailhead, a short walk up to a ridge with big rock formations. His body began to move without thought. He walked toward the main roadway. When he arrived there, he felt a defiance arise in him. He'd told Sequoia he would meet her at the airport, but he had no experience of the area; he didn't know how long it would take. He walked to the right shoulder of the road and started to hitchhike. The first car to approach stopped for him.

"We're going to Two Trees," the passenger hollered. "That work for you?"

Teuton was unfamiliar with the roads and had no idea what Two Trees was, but he thought there could only be one roadway from town. The defiance he was feeling was such an alive feeling for him, he didn't bother to check in with the gentle, subtle, knowing, in the moment. Besides, he would be on his way to somewhere and independent of the whole dependence on Sequoia.

"Sure!"

He climbed into the rear passenger door. Three people were already in the car, and immediately the introductions and conversation about visiting Sedona started. Teuton didn't notice when they passed a tee in the road; riding in the limo he'd come in with Sequoia, he had been looking all around and not paying attention to the road. He assumed the road to town would be straight from the resort. Within a few miles, the road became dirt and gravel. He didn't remember that, but riding in a small car would be very different from a big heavy limo, so he reasoned it was possible he didn't notice.

The ride became more unfamiliar. The gravel road arrived at a tee, and the driver turned right. Conversation was lively; the people were from New York. They had been there three days and eagerly talked about the hikes they'd taken. The road went on and on. Teuton just relegated the situation to the universe, doing exactly what needed to be done in perfection.

They turned into the Honanki Ruins parking lot. "Hey, we've heard about this place," the driver declared. "Let's check it out."

Teuton began to feel the pressure of making a mistake. The sun was about an hour from sunset, depending upon what Sequoia would think sunset was. For him, it could be anywhere in a ninety-minute window, depending on the cloud conditions. He had no idea what Sequoia would think the time of sunset was. There were other cars in the parking lot.

When they got out of the car, Teuton thanked the driver for the ride and told him he needed to get to an appointment in Sedona, so he'd wait behind and see if someone else could give him a ride. As they headed off to the ruins, he approached a young couple who were just getting back to their car.

"Hey, are you going back to Sedona?" Teuton asked them.

"No, but we're going back to Enchantment," the young woman replied. They were giddishly in love and didn't seem to want to have company.

"Thanks anyway," Teuton replied. "I need to get to the Sedona Airport."

He watched as the car left the parking lot and wondered if he'd passed up the best chance he'd get. There was a brightly painted truck from a company named Pink Jeep. There was one more car. Teuton decided to take the trail and catch up with the New Yorkers, see what the ruin was, and continue with them.

He walked the whole trail, looping back to the parking lot without seeing anyone else. The ruins were interesting, but he hurried by them, feeling pressed for time. When he arrived back, all the cars were gone and the gate to the parking lot had been closed! He decided to walk back to the main road, but when he arrived there, he didn't know which direction to go. He watched the sun begin to dip into the horizon. There were no lights of civilization in any direction, only aircraft flying at full cruising altitude. He pulled his coat closer to his neck and finished bringing the zipper up.

If only I knew which way to go, he thought, *I could walk and stay warm. It was a long way out here. Is this the way things are supposed to work out?* His thoughts began to reason with themselves for lack of someone to talk about the situation with. *I wonder what's going on with Sequoia. All my belongings are in Salt Lake City, in my car at the bank. This is pretty desolate and far from civilization. I wonder what animals are out here? I don't have a flashlight, food, or anything but my wallet, some change, my comb, and car keys. What good are car keys without my car? Just how screwed am I?*

Sequoia paid and tipped the driver and then turned toward the terminal doors. The place seemed dark. She tugged on the door. It was locked. The hours weren't posted. She decided to circle the terminal to look for Teuton. She walked around the terminal and then looked out toward her airplane. There was a restaurant near her parking place. She decided to go to the restaurant to see if Teuton might be waiting there.

As daylight faded, Teuton heard the barking of large dogs. He decided to walk down the road toward the sounds. He hoped dogs meant a ranch house or something. Besides, walking would keep him warm and give him purpose.

Well after dark, Teuton's walk paid off. He saw lights and buildings and followed them to the ranch. When he arrived, he didn't see any vehicles, but there was a house with lights on. The dogs were giving plenty of warning of his approach. If anyone was in the house, he would have thought they would come to the door to investigate why the dogs were making such a ruckus. He watched the dogs carefully as he inched his way toward the house. They were bigger than he expected and looked like wolves. At the door, he knocked.

A voice came from nearby: "Who are you ... why are you here?"

Teuton looked around. He wanted to know which direction to talk.

"My name is Teuton and I'm lost. I needed to get to Sedona Airport. I need some help."

"I ain't got a car," the female voice said, "and I ain't got a phone. Where's your car?"

"I'm here without a car. It's a complicated story. I've never been to Sedona before today. I had lunch at Enchantment Resort and hitch-hiked but the guys didn't know where they were going, then I got left at a ruin back an hour's walk or so. I was supposed to meet my ride at the airport terminal at sunset."

"I've got a gun. My girlfriend works until closing. She'll be home about midnight. Go over to the barn and let yourself in. You can keep warm there. If I find you're snooping around the house again, I'll use this gun. Don't test me!"

Teuton thought to himself, *What a mess. I need shelter. This woman is afraid being out here all alone. And another woman coming? That's my only hope for a ride? Wonder what's going on with Sequoia. Is she's flying off somewhere right now? Where's the barn door? Is there some lesson in this? I've got to get through the night.*

Sequoia couldn't calm herself enough to get clear in the moment. Her thoughts raced: *I thought he'd be there. What happened to him? I really fucked up. What was I thinking to kidnap a guy and think he'd be okay with it? What if he's gone to the police and reported me for kidnapping? What am I going to do for the night? I could take off and fly to somewhere VFR where I won't be traceable. The restaurant closed. The signs say no overnight camping. What if he comes back and I'm gone? He's going to be even angrier. He's got no right to be angry with me, look at all I've been doing for him. He has every right in the world to be angry with me. He's been violated. What was I thinking?*

She walked over to the Sky Ranch Lodge to see about getting a room. *If the plane is there when Teuton comes back, at least he'll know I'm still around. It's getting too cold. I've got to have shelter.*

She got a room at Sky Ranch. When she entered the room, she thought how this might be more comfortable for Teuton than what she was accustomed to. Why did she fail to realize she needed to connect with him and work things out together? Then she thought of going back to the office, making a sign, and putting it on the plane, telling Teuton which room he could find her in. That was the best idea in hours, she thought, as she busied herself with making a sign.

Teuton searched in the dark barn for something comfortable and warm. He could hold up until the other woman came at midnight. He might get a ride to Sedona or at least get a couch to sleep on, out of the cold night. He found a place to hunker down and wait. It was January, and the mountains of Arizona get well into freezing at night. Staying warm while waiting was the best he could do.

Hours later: The dogs barked, sounding excited to see someone, and the sound of a car arriving brought hope to Teuton. He was shivering now, and his toes were numb. He needed to get out the door and be noticed as the driver was coming in, not to startle her. So as quick as he could walk after being bundled up, and with cold toes, he made his way into the light of the oncoming car.

As the car came to a stop, the driver left the headlights on after turning off the engine and rolled down her window. "Who are you?" a woman said. "What you doing here?"

He walked toward the car.

"Stop right there." He heard the sound of a gun being cocked. "Why are you here?"

Teuton realized he needed good answers. "I've been here for hours. I talked to the woman in the house, and she said I could wait in the barn. My name is Teuton, and I'm damn cold. I was supposed to be at Sedona Airport at sunset."

"You fucking what? There's no airport out here." Her voice was slurred.

"I hitched a ride with some idiots that took me way out here," he reported.

"Didn't you know where you were? Did they roll you too? Do you have any money?" she asked as Teuton began to get enough information to realize he was reasoning with someone under the influence of chemicals.

"I have a little money. I can pay for a ride to Sedona Airport. Can I sleep on a couch and catch a ride when you go back into town tomorrow?" he asked.

"No, you can't, Mister. But this is your lucky night, 'cause I just came back to take my girlfriend to a party in town. I'll give you a ride to town."

Teuton wasn't comfortable with the idea of riding with someone under the influence, but they weren't going to give him shelter, and it was his best option to accept the ride. "Okay. I appreciate that. Can I get into the car and get warm?"

"You got cash, grass, or ass, 'cause you ain't riding for free," she said, giggling at her cleverness. "Get in the car. I'll go get my girl."

The ride to the airport was eventful. He realized the driver had survived driving in her condition before, but he wasn't sure he would. When they got to the airport terminal, only the area lights were on. The buildings of the terminal and restaurant were dark. Teuton saw Sequoia's plane on the tarmac. He'd warmed up on the trip into town, but it was probably in the single digits outside. He thanked the women, gave them two twenty-dollar bills, and waved as they drove away.

He stopped to ponder the past eighteen hours of his life. It still wasn't over, but at least the plane was still there, so Sequoia might have left a note or something. Perhaps she was in the plane, but it would be a refrigerator. So he walked to the plane and found the note on the ground with a tape that obviously didn't stick. The light wasn't good enough to read the note, so he walked back to an area light.

It was 3:20 a.m. when Sequoia heard a knock at the door of her room. She hadn't undressed, staying ready in case she got news of Teuton. She rushed to the door and opened it without caution. When she saw Teuton standing there, all the tension and anxiety she'd been consumed by melted away.

"Come in," she blurted out. "It's so cold out there!"

Teuton came in and closed the door. He stood shivering.

"Here, I'll turn up the heat. What happened to you?" Sequoia asked.

"A continuation of the weirdest twenty hours of my life," he replied. "I don't want to talk about the story right now. How are you doing?"

"I've been in transformation," she said meekly. "I've really been taking a look at the assumptions I live with. I put on your moccasins and started walking. I want to talk with you, if you're awake enough."

"May I sit? I mean, I'm in a woman's hotel room. I'd like permission to make myself at home. May I?"

"Oh, I'm sorry, of course. There's a bed here for you. Are you okay with sleeping in the same room? I realize it is presumptuous on my part; I keep being presumptuous. It's my way of life, but I want you to know I'm taking responsibility for it and how it makes it difficult for you to relate with me."

Teuton felt his heart soften. "I did some of my own inner work," he said. "I don't understand what loving you is about for me, but I want to communicate with you and find our balance so I can be clearer about why we're together. I realize we aren't together, but somehow we are, and I don't understand it."

Sequoia felt a safety as she heard him speak of love for her. She felt it too. It seemed more real for him to confess it as something he didn't understand and yet had the courage to talk about it. "Amigo, I don't know either. You've challenged me like no one ever has, exactly with the proficiencies you've mastered. You're directly honest with me. Do you know I've never had that: someone who expects me to accept him as my equal and hits me with his honesty for me to deal with as I may, take it or leave it?"

He shared, "It took some time to see that I have the same energy as you do. I mean that lifetimes before this one, I lived in privilege and massive abundance. It's in me every bit as much as it is in you. I even see that I have dragged along with me an image of myself someone else wanted me to have, instead of being myself. I have done all this transformation work but didn't bother to update the image I keep of myself."

She replied, "I've seen some yucky flaws in my perfect world. I have never, ever really been receptive, been vulnerable, and waited for anything meaningful in my life. People have always been so eager to please me."

She paused and then continued, "At sunset, I was here. I already knew I had to wait for you, and you may never come, but I realized you're important enough to do something I couldn't even imagine myself being able to do. Then you didn't come. My worries and insecurities kept me so involved, I couldn't back out of them and be in the moment to know the truth of the moment. I was so wrapped up in thoughts about what I didn't know and couldn't understand; I was a mess."

She paused again, this time leaning toward Teuton.

"I saw my weakness and became vulnerable. I have stories about how it is I love you, but they are past, and I need to get into now, here now, with loving you. I need my now truth. I care about you enough to look deeply within myself and see what I need to own; I haven't wanted to see that before. I have been playing it out intolerably with you, and you've shown me you must be respected and loved in more grown-up ways."

"I've done all that?" Teuton asked, somewhat frivolously.

Sequoia felt herself bristle at his mocking her. "No, you haven't. But you would walk, no run, away from everything I could offer you if you didn't feel an equality between us. I saw that. I saw that in myself when I looked at me from walking in your moccasins."

Teuton went into his inner truth of the moment. "Okay, since you've shared that, I have seen how I wasn't being an equal and wasn't accepting being whatever you've been used to in people, either. And I saw you as my equal, someone I want to teeter back and forth through the balance point with. That teetering might be a lot of struggle until we break our old habits and get it working well. I'm promising you a messy partnership, whatever we do together."

Sequoia muffled her yelling so as not to disturb anyone in an adjacent room: "You so piss me off, Teuton! You're proud, arrogant, determined, and you won't kiss my ass. That's exactly what I need until I develop into a grown-up relationship with you ... whatever that becomes."

"Whatever that becomes? Are you willing to reconsider your being beyond sex? Is that included in 'whatever that becomes'?" Teuton asked defiantly.

"Why would you want to make love with me? You'd just get exclusive and miss out on all the other lovers who enjoy you. I'd become your one-and-only, not because you believe in it, but because ..."

Teuton interrupted, "Because what? Because we already have the capacity to go further, to go deeper with each other? Is it because we have made love so many times in our lifetimes, it would be comfortable, like where we always belonged? Would we simply forget there are others to be lovers with? What's your story, amiga?"

"You think I just have stories?" Sequoia shot back at him with fire in her eyes. "I have stories because they tell about what's inside me that can't have words and explanations without stories, that's why stories, and yes, I have stories."

"Fine," he spouted back. "Just go on telling your stories, your fictions that protect you from intimacy. When you're begging and hot with desire to make love with me, I am going to coldly insist I'm beyond what you long for and leave you wondering what the truth is of my stand with you."

"When I'm ready, if I ever am, you'll be the last to get the memo. You're such an insensitive prick. You just want the victory of laying me." Sequoia was growing more furious.

"I already have the victory," he said, relentlessly prodding her. "You're afraid to go there with me. You're afraid to let go and explore your passion. I know it's there, but you think you're beyond it."

"It doesn't matter what I am," she spat, "I have the right to have my boundaries. I don't have to explain and justify them, and by damn, you better be respectful of my boundaries. They're my boundaries, and that is all you need to know. As long as I have them, they're there to be honored and respected."

"Well, Miss 'Just Friends,' amiga, lover of many lifetimes, the time will come when you'll so regret all your boundaries. And who knows, you may decide to relax your boundaries and find your window of opportunity passed." He wagged his finger at her.

"Is this what you call being equals, to meet me head on with the most sensitive of issues?" Sequoia's voice broke into crying as she protested in muffled tones.

"Put yourself completely into everything else about being and working together and make it better than lovemaking," Teuton said, hardly understanding why he was saying such things.

"Gawd! It doesn't matter what form you can possess me, you want to possess me!" with exasperation and sarcasm streaming in her voice.

"Touché! How does it feel to have someone want to possess you? That is how you started with me, completely taking me over and possessing me. How do you like it?" Teuton felt so self-assured as he pushed her into a sampling of what he felt she'd been doing.

"Well, I'll tell you one thing, and listen well: I'll never make love with you until I feel it isn't about power, isn't about possessing, isn't about making a point, and is, hear me say this, *is* about expressing passionate desire to merge completely in love for each other." Sequoia sounded defiant, not letting him have one-upmanship with her.

"Agreed," Teuton countered. "Not until, not one moment before you know you love me and want to merge with me because you can't stand another minute of hiding from it."

"Okay, agreed. I'm calling the front desk to extend another day. This bed is mine. It is the only place you may not sleep. There, I haven't tried to own, possess, mother, or in any other way control-freak you."

"I'll try not to disturb you. I'm taking a shower. I've been in a dark dusty barn with who knows what for warmth and comfort."

"Good night, amigo. I really do love you."

Teuton couldn't answer that. She'd found his sensitive spot and had the last word.

Chapter 5

———~∿∽◦◦﹏◦◦∽∿———

Calivigny Island, Grenada

"Wow, I love how synchronicity works," Teuton said. "I can't imagine being any more excited about living than this moment. We're here to create something new, a model of life to first of all serve who we are. We've been out there seeing how different our proficiencies have made us from society. We can't be so different and live in these societies. In respect for the world around us, and taking care of ourselves, we have the opportunity to establish an international community, strengthening who we are so we can lead the world into what's possible. We are what's possible, and now is the time to take it to the next level." He was speaking at the opening of a community meeting on the beautiful resort island of Calivigny.

Teuton and Sequoia made their way there after leaving Sedona. It was the place Sequoia wanted to share with Teuton. Synchronicity had completely filled the resort with people who had also developed their proficiencies with them. They felt deeply connected with the community of people from the island.

It was Sequoia's turn to speak: "From a discussion some of us had last night, we've identified five areas of life we want steering committees to meet and develop. We ask you to choose the one that appeals most to you.

"The first committee will work on what our community will look like in the world. Please determine what we can do to live together and yet not be isolated from the world.

87

"The second committee will work on establishing our intent, our mission statement. I know that seems like the first thing. We already have a sense of it. We just need to clarify that we're all on the same page. It isn't about inventing it, it is about discovering it within our collective.

"The third committee will develop our model for raising our children. Some already have children, so we need a model that incorporates those kids and those who are born here.

"The fourth committee will work on our education system; everyone in our community will participate in education as a lifelong process.

"And the fifth committee will work on how we're going to use our resources to collect all the beneficial information of our planet we want to incorporate into our new society. We're living it and preparing it to give to the entire planet's way of life. I can hardly wait to see what you come up with.

"There are materials in each of your meeting rooms. No leaders have been chosen. You'll start with the idea, and each group will develop their own competencies."

"Now let us end this session in silence," Teuton concluded, "so we can each know."

This was the first time Teuton and Sequoia worked together in leadership. He was stretching himself in realization of the whole picture of his lifetimes of evolution, not forgetting this lifetime's experience but seeing how it was a boot camp to serve who he is for his whole evolution. Once he realized the whole picture, the micro experience of earlier in this lifetime had a place, and he was free to move forward as himself, as a continuity.

For Sequoia, being reunited with her partner of many lifetimes was more complete and empowering than she'd ever felt, even though she was also having to get in touch with a continuity of lifetimes to help her break habits of how she related to people in this lifetime. Something in her knew how to meet her partner in equality, even if she'd never done so in this lifetime. She simply connected with what she wasn't recognizing that was herself through combined lifetimes. For her, too, this lifetime was a microcosm that had a place in the whole of her evolution.

It wasn't such a struggle for either of them, when they let go of this lifetime being the center of their experience. As with all other lifetimes, the moment was the only place anything existed, and they could live the moment most effectively by accepting all that had been their evolution in living in moment.

A group of twenty participants had gathered; they had enthusiasm for what they might do to contribute to life on the planet, particularly how they might help humanity survive a worldwide calamity.

The intimacy and depth of connection was evident as they first met hugging, holding, and settling in a puppy pile of affection and comfort with each other. It was easy for them to connect and be affectionate with one another. They'd overcome jealousy and exclusivity, opening their hearts to accepting and loving each other in every way. They were free of energy bundles, imprints, and the programming that makes relationships messy.

They arrived at a moment where the focus and energy went to one person: Viplow. He saw everyone looking his way and knew he was chosen to lead the group. Everyone else knew, too: he was to take responsibility.

Viplow shuffled to his feet, surveyed the materials left in the room, and thought of the need for someone to record. His eyes went to Ashwini. She stirred and looked around to see everyone looking at her. She let go of the hands she was holding and hopped to her feet. Then all eyes went to Jaing. She knew she was chosen to write on the easel and wiggled free of her cuddle with friends.

"Thank you," Viplow started. "Think of all the doomsday predictions and movies about catastrophic changes that might transition all of life on the planet. What do we want to do for our way of life to be the one that reseeds the planet? What could we do so humanity could benefit from all that's been accomplished and not have to take centuries to rediscover what we've already developed?"

Antonio, living in the role of aeronautical engineer, spoke first, saying, "The idea of something on land isn't foolproof. Making some kind of community under the surface of the ocean has interesting merits, but if something happened to cause rapid shifts in the water, it might not survive. Winds can have tremendous force on the surface, and shock waves in air are just as destructive as moving water; they carry energy from water and earth movements. However, at high altitudes, the air is thin; disturbances in the air are not so powerful and dissipate quickly. We can't place static structures at high altitudes, but we could build and man a space station, which wouldn't be disturbed by the forces on earth."

Lilian interjected, "That's complicated and expensive. We'd have a lot of limitations of how much we could transport material back and forth to the surface. How about using airplanes? We could have enough of them to always have some flying should something happen. That could be done more easily, and there's been prototypes developed of engines that work with energy all around us that has promise of keeping an airplane flying indefinitely."

Jaing wrote "Airplanes with new technology" on the easel.

"Together, we have the resources to put anything together we want," Zeke said. "What if we develop in stages? First, we can bring stuff into warehouses. Then as we get airplanes and equip them with the ability to fly without depending on fossil fuels, we can transfer what we've gathered into the planes. Meanwhile, we can work on engineering and making a space station we can move resources into. Eventually, we could equip vehicles in the seas, in the air, and in space."

Lilian spoke again: "These are the things governments usually do. We've got the advantage that we've got more resources; we're a planetary community in cohesion with each other, and we can act without bureaucracies. We'll simply do it."

Jaing wrote "Submarines," "Warehouses," and "Space station" on the easel.

"Okay," Viplow redirected, "what do we want to preserve? What do we want these vehicles to preserve?"

Vickie volunteered, "I know what I *don't* want to preserve. I don't want information about weapons or antiquated systems of injustice, exploitation, or power to be preserved. Let's give peace and love a chance to be the basis for life."

"I agree," Viplow said. "With that being said, what *do* we want? What inventions, what information, what foods, what medicines, what practices do we trust will establish life on the planet like never before? Let's list what will be beyond what does not serve our collective well-being."

At that, the committee became enthusiastic and spouted out many ideas, keeping Jaing and Ashwini busy recording them all.

"Good morning, amigo," Sequoia said, greeting Teuton.

"Good morning."

"Did you get any sleep? You were sure enjoying the ladies last night," she continued.

"Yeah," he replied, "I don't ever want to be beyond connecting deeply with others and pleasuring them. I can't imagine anything better."

"I used to go there," she declared. "It is *so* out of my system now."

"You keep saying that," Teuton continued. "We've got committees reporting this morning. Have you had any thoughts?"

"I had interest in the committee discussing our mission, our intentions. They came up with an interesting statement. It was all about being a fluid community with our energies spread around the planet; everyone would travel to different sub-communities and raise our children in entirely different ways, in the safety of the communities, and expose them to the regular world, coaching them in being conscious. They had strong feelings about living our lifestyles, getting them established well, and expanding to those who are drawn to us."

"So they will integrate the island experience into everyday life and establish a web of communities that make up one worldwide community?" he asked, wanting to know if he was getting a sense of what she was describing.

"Sure. When we get going, I'm going to be watching for the synchronicities. The pieces of the puzzle will be fun to watch coming together."

"Are you up for brunch?" Teuton asked. "I'm hungry."

"Go ahead," she replied. "I'll join you. I have a small project."

There was no appointed time to begin the meeting. As the participants had a sense of expediency for the meeting, they went to the meeting room. It was about five minutes from the arrival of the first participant to the arrival of the last.

"Welcome back. Is everyone enjoying being together?" Teuton led with.

There was an enthusiastic crowd noise in response.

"Any business before we hear from each committee?" Sequoia asked.

Jana spoke up: "Let's knock off between three and four so we have plenty of time for beach play before our evening meal."

A murmur of consensus followed.

"Okay, we're in agreement. Anything else?" Sequoia said.

"Will we be implementing our ideas?" Sudheer asked.

"The energy is already moving that way. Let's all take a minute and connect with the energy we're feeling present," Teuton suggested. "Let it communicate with you and sense how we can begin to make decisions in its flow."

Jasmine was sitting in front of Teuton. Her silky dark hair shimmered in the sunlight, catching his attention. He felt excitement surge in his body as he tried not to see through her sheer dress. Their eyes met. For a few moments, they gazed into each other's depths of being. Teuton felt his breath shorten and his cheeks flush. She winked at him while giving a flirtatious smile.

"Jasmine, please tell us what your committee came up with," Teuton said as he tried to direct attention away from his attraction to her.

Sequoia saw what was going on. Her attention to Teuton had become important to her, and without realizing she was doing so, she often found herself keeping tabs on what he was up to. She wasn't so sure how she felt about Jasmine and Teuton being interested in each other. Still, she had to allow him to express what she was sure she was beyond. She was practicing giving up what she'd begun their relationship with, being controlling with Teuton. She suspected he was sensitive to any nuances of control she might exhibit; allowing Teuton the freedom to enjoy his lovers put her in a quandary. After all, she'd had many lovers in her pathway to being done with sex. She couldn't impose celibacy on Teuton, but something in her wanted him exclusively. Where she believed herself to be wouldn't let her have him like the other women did.

"Sure, I just happen to be the spokeswoman for my group." Jasmine's words broke the chain of Sequoia's thought stream. "We came up with how we think we can best make a lifestyle around who we are."

Jasmine grinned as she walked past Teuton to take a microphone and pick up a marker for the easel. Teuton felt excitement rushing through his body, sensing the grin was her delight at how she engaged Teuton's attraction. At five feet eleven inches tall, her athletic body had a nice figure, and her legs were pleasing to the eye.

"We all know that clearing away the energy of old stuff, neutralizing the media programming, and developing our competencies has made us different from the people we're around who haven't shared our experiences. We want to establish a lifestyle around that and at the same time not make any walls, psychologically or physically, that prevent a healthy flow of energy. There's a balance we want to teeter with."

Teuton enjoyed every movement Jasmine was making and her brilliance as she presented. He wasn't noticing Sequoia was more intent on him than the presentation.

Jasmine continued, "We also want to be global. We represent all races and most nationalities in loving harmony." (She emphasized the word "loving" as she spoke.) "We want to establish communities throughout the world we can all live in. It isn't that we find a community and stay in it. These communities will be fluid. That means we come and go from one community to another, enjoying the synchronicities of whoever else happens to be staying where we are."

She walked over and handed the marker to Sam. "Sam, would you please write words to remind us of our points on the easel? I can't talk and write and maintain my thoughts as well.

"Our communities will not be isolated households yet will have rooms, patios, and meditation gardens for time alone," she continued. "Generally, we will continue to live much as we did on the island."

She glanced at Sequoia and noticed she wasn't following her; she didn't catch her reference to the island. She was noticing a vulnerability in Sequoia she hadn't seen before.

"We will need to be set apart from the neighbors and world around us," she added, "just because we can't have them seeing how we live. It won't work to have them know our lifestyle is so free and different from theirs."

Sequoia interrupted, "We know we're different. That's the whole point. How do you propose to help the world move into sharing what we share?"

"Thank you for asking," Jasmine replied gracefully and sincerely. "We know it doesn't help the poor to become poor. We need to have our community and support system strongly in force for us while we move and associate with people in the marketplace, so to speak. There's a balance of being set apart with walls for safety and to prevent being watched, and at the same time living in a way our being resonates with others in a way that sparks a desire to develop what they experience in us for themselves. It will require living our competencies with consciousness. Does that add clarity?"

Sequoia nodded her head affirmatively.

Jasmine continued, "We can't dictate a bunch of rules for how we'll live. Our competencies are the best guides for that. We'll know. It will be easier to continue building strength in our competencies, living in a community with each other. Naturally, we want each community to have amenities for playfulness and enjoyment. We need to school our children. When we move to another community, we just take our personal belongings and know that when we arrive at the next community, what we need will be there. We all leave behind what isn't personal for others to enjoy using."

Then Jasmine looked to Teuton, both giving him the message her presentation was done and continuing the flow of sexual delight between them.

Teuton stood, turned, and addressed everyone: "Can we defer questions and discussion until all the presentations are done?" There was a murmur of approval, and each person raised a hand in affirmation.

"Thank you, beloved," Teuton said to Jasmine as he put his arm around her and kissed her while escorting her out of the limelight. Sam pulled the easel sheets he'd written over the top to reveal a blank paper for the next presentation.

Sequoia took her turn to conduct the meeting. She walked over to Taj, reaching her hand to help him to his feet. When he was standing his full six feet, she wrapped her arms around his neck and kissed him. Then she led him to the front of the room.

Teuton watched in surprise. He'd never seen Sequoia be that flirtatious. He felt a bit perplexed and began to wonder if there were others who Sequoia shared intimacy with. For certain, she didn't share it with him. He yearned for her to kiss him that way.

Taj was from India, with jet black hair and deep brown eyes that glowed in warmth and excitement to be alive. He took the microphone.

"I am so full of gratitude to be with all of you. You're my soul family, and I love you, each and every one of you.

"We've got children. We're going to have more children. We want to raise them competently and consciously so they grow in the world we're leading the way into. We want them to be educated in a natural way. We want them to be full of excitement and gratitude for life.

"When a woman decides she wants to have a child, she will make preparation to conceive in consciousness. She'll trust that the men who are in the community with her at the time are the right ones to father her baby. She won't be exclusive, so unless we were to do DNA testing on all the men, we won't know who the father is. This will be good, because it is every man's responsibility to treat each child as his, giving his fatherly qualities to each child. Testing could spoil that. Even if a man knows he couldn't be the father to a child, he will still treat each child as his.

"This will be healthy for the children, to have many parents caring for them. If their mom is unavailable, they'll be accustomed to having many parents to fill their needs. In the same way, every woman will nurture and care for other children as her own. It may be the natural mother is better at some needed skill and not so patient with children, but other women will attract kids to her mothering gifts. The children will flow freely with the adults around them, trusting their world as a safe place with many resources to draw upon.

"We expect children to be more curious and intelligent, developing more relating skills with the variety of how adults model and share with them. We have experienced how children are more secure and cooperative with each other. They're also comfortable with nurturing and being appropriately affectionate with one another.

"The children's sexuality will be celebrated and encouraged as they grow. They will know sexuality as a normal part of relating, as they will freely mingle with adults who are being affectionate and sexual with each other. We'll be mindful of allowing them to explore sexuality with each other, allowing and encouraging them to be sexual within an equality of age and experience, openly, in the presence of adults and peers, as always protecting the girls from pregnancy until they're adults and ready to consciously bear children.

"As the children reach the age where they shift more to relating with peers, they'll travel in escorted groups between communities, independent of their mothers.

"We'll expose our children to people in general, all the while educating them and coaching them in developing skills for relating at the level the general population will be okay with, so they can consciously live in both worlds."

"Wow, Taj, that's really beautiful," Sequoia said as she rose to her feet. "I bet we all wish we'd been raised that way. What a bunch of lucky kids." She walked to Taj, put her arm around his waist, and spoke as she looked around the group: "How many of you had your sexuality encouraged and celebrated and knew what it was all about by being around it as a natural way people relate?

"How many of you learned to trust the world by every adult being a parent for you? Imagine having so many adults to help develop your own unique gifts, to model different possibilities for you."

Taj added, "Some of us have studied tribal societies. They weren't tainted by the world as we know it. In many ways, we've become untainted so we believe we can and must live as they have. Except for knowing the ways of the outside world, they're ahead of us in personal well-being. We want to incorporate what we've learned with their lifestyles into living in the modern world. We propose to be the meeting of both."

"Thank you, Taj," Sequoia announced for everyone.

Teuton stood and said, "That flows naturally to go right into what we want to consider for our education system."

Elekcia stood and walked to the front of the group. She gave Teuton a hug and kiss, and then she stood with her arm around him as she addressed everyone.

"We learn from everyone. I was there when Teuton arrived on the island. He wasn't a promising candidate, and I for one, just walked away, keeping my distance for a while. He was eager to develop himself, and he gave back to all of us in return.

"Most of all, we want our education system to give meaning to the concept expressed in the word 'love.' We know love is a lifelong education and the basis of divinity. We know that a strong heart presence enables us, in too many ways to think of trying to count them.

"We want our education system to acknowledge that education is an ongoing process that, for all we know, may begin before our births and may continue after leaving our bodies."

Then Elekcia gave Teuton a deep, melting hug and finished with a deep passionate kiss. Everyone cheered.

She continued, "So learning to love openly, has been a struggle for most of us, but we've grown. We want to educate our children in loving one another and being able to enjoy the many expressions of love, also learning to be appropriate in the moment. I am happy the previous presentation addressed this.

"So we want to embrace the Waldorf system. We want everyone to learn enough about teaching that we are all resources to our children and each other. We propose everyone learn to be Waldorf educators. We're already mostly there. We can be more conscious and intentional about it.

"Is there anyone here who feels they were educated in the foundation of loving presence?"

There was a murmur among everyone, but no one spoke up.

The Elekcia asked everyone, "How many of you hated having to go to school?" Most of the hands went up.

Addressing the consensus, she went on, "We want education to be so natural, our children wonder what we're talking about when we mention school. We want them to learn subject matter, becoming well-informed and developing their intelligence. We want them to be competent, with the same competencies of life skills we all are growing into.

"There won't be experts running the show. Those with the most expertise will coach others in taking responsibility and leadership, being in the shadow as consultants rather than running things. This means we learn, and I mean we of all ages, learn through stepping into our subject matter; even though we don't know at first what we're doing, we'll do it as real as possible as we grow into it. That makes it imperative to learn as we need what we're learning in real-life applications."

Elekcia started walking around, and then she wandered through the audience. "Some of you may be thinking things will be messy. That's right. And as students, we'll learn through the messiness. Getting messy is a great teacher. Then, as students become adept at mastering a subject, if someone wants to learn, they become teachers from the shadows.

"This is about giving what we've received, which is another step of education: the step when we become masters of our subjects. When we can watch and coach others in becoming proficient at something, it deepens our abilities too.

"Taking charge and being in charge is for novices. Just look at Teuton, working with and learning from Sequoia. She's been our example, but she stays mostly in the shadows so the rest of us can grow into our own empowerment.

"Teuton, I want to acknowledge that you offer just as much to Sequoia, with what you bring to her and the rest of us, as any of us offer you. You're valuable to us, and we love you."

Teuton shifted his body shyly as he received the recognition. Sequoia listened deeply to the message, realizing Teuton was being declared her equal by another leader of the community she'd led. Was he being elevated to guru status, or was her belief she had guru status not shared? Sequoia felt uneasy and challenged. Upon witnessing herself in the moment, she knew the layers of inequality between her and Teuton would evolve into the light for some time.

Elekcia was a teacher and accustomed to speaking for a long time; she continued, "I know we have a lot to put together, and everything we do is our education, so it continues to evolve; it is already underway.

"I also want to remind us of another important element of our education system: That is sensing the flow of where life is going and being in harmony with ... going with the flow. We need to be that, always returning to consciousness of where the flow is going when we get into distraction. We want to teach and learn the balance between making something happen and the flow being where things evolve with the most ease.

"'Respond-ability' is the outcome of our education: the ability to respond to what is going on. No one person will have all the ability. To recognize what team members are needed for their strengths and talents is wisdom.

"We want our education system to convey wisdom. Wisdom cannot be taught, but it can be modeled, and it will come to those who are open and receptive while at the same time developing their unique contributions to themselves and life."

Then Elekcia stood and looked around the room, making eye contact with each person present, one at a time. Everyone remained silent. Then she made eye contact with Sequoia. Both Sequoia's and Elekcia's eyes filled with tears, and they met each other in a melting hug, sharing a meaningful kiss before they parted. Elekcia put her arm around Sequoia's waist and motioned for Teuton to come to her other side. Holding them both around the waist, Elekcia looked at the floor for a few moments with her head bowed, and then she slowly raised her head and looked again at everyone.

"In deep gratitude," Elekcia said, "You're my family, and not just my family but my friends, the family I choose for myself. I've cried with you, I've screamed with you, I've danced with you, I've played with you, we've been naked together without need for special status, and we've made love together. You've all been my teachers, as I have opened myself as I never imagined I could. We're there for each other, and we know we can share anything, because we've practiced sharing even our most vulnerable and intimate moments with each other.

"When I look within for the love I have for each one of you, it is so magnificent and beyond anything I could have dreamed of. I feel like one radiating star of gratitude. You're the greatest gift, the greatest possession, the greatest privilege, the greatest honor I could ever conceive of.

"What our committee is proposing is that we all continue growing in what we already have. Our education will overflow with abundance in every way, so amazing our children will naturally immerse themselves in our abundance.

"Please take a minute to go into the wordless energy field so I can share with you what words cannot describe."

Sequoia felt so moved by Elekcia's appeal to the group, she knew the right thing to do in the moment was to quietly end for the day. She walked over to the easel and wrote, "Session over for today. Play in the sun and surf. Great food tonight, and love party into the wee hours."

CHAPTER 6

———~wooeᴛⱺⱻᴛꞓᴏⱺwᴡ———

Eight years later.

It was just before dusk. The air was crisp as a 787 Dreamliner rested on the tarmac, undergoing its preflight inspection. The air stirred with a welcome steady breeze, blowing the usual winter smog out of the area. The noise of the rush-hour traffic was a steady droning, with bursts of jet blasts as planes took off, one after another. At the moment, the traffic of both was heavier than usual.

This aircraft was owned by the world's largest airline, operated exclusively by members of C-Know. It was officially a division for research, only known for what it really is by the airline's board of directors. Sequoia's family were the largest stockholders, so the board answered to the managers of the family trust. Being within a massive business structure concealed the operations, and whatever was needed for the mission of C-Know could easily be purchased and handled through the umbrella of the airline.

It wasn't secrecy but invisibility that protected C-Know, for secrecy invited penetration. If C-Know were not invisible, it would be fodder for the media and potentially be stormed by masses of people desperate to be preserved after whatever calamities they believed in. It was simply not a wise option to make C-Know general knowledge.

The aircraft was equipped exactly like the six other Dreamliners. It was modified to withstand exceptional forces, its communication systems designed to survive every possible scenario the makers could imagine, including exceptional intensity from the sun or from massive atomic explosions. It was able to detect and process information beyond the capability of a common commercial aircraft. To compensate pilots for its limited visibility, it had cameras built into the exterior, providing an extra sphere of visibility. Its radar capacities were extended to the rear, to the top, and underneath. It had sensors to detect and measure radiation. It had sensors to see light spectrums not visible to human eyes. It had the latest technology to sense and read energy patterns, pulses, and so on.

As most people know, a pilot's workstation is very complex. An additional station, much like the old navigator's station from before electronic navigation, was built into the aircraft, with seating for two to work with the additional input of information to assist the pilots.

The little-known additional jet engine that generated power for all of the systems inside the planes was replaced by motors made per patents that had been bought up to keep the fossil fuel industry going. They didn't consume fuel, had no emissions, and operated steadily at no cost. The right to develop the designs was granted under specific legal agreements, preventing any other uses. The agreements also demanded the condition of invisibility. The aircraft simply did not exist, except to qualified personnel with high security clearance. Again, Sequoia's family and friends were invaluable resources, and in fact, they had all developed their proficiencies through Sequoia's island project.

The outboard engines used technology to begin the process of preparing energy before it came into the engine, then electronically exciting the energy under compression, causing instant expansion without oxidation, which increased the energetic presence from 500 to 3,000 times the space it occupies, causing more thrust than jet fuel. The energy rapidly contracted to its original space behind the plane without any known change to the original state of the energy. A common nickname for this type of energy was Zero Point Energy, yet all other atoms and compounds in the air also expanded their energetic presence. Because water wasn't formed through combustion of fossil fuel, the planes left no contrails. The expansion was hotter than jet fuel but quickly cooled as it left the engine.

The power of the engines were calibrated to perform the same as other jet fueled Dreamliners, so pilots experienced in those aircraft would not have to be specially checked out. Computers operated the engines based on pilot or autopilot settings. However, the engines had reserve power that could compensate for exceptional conditions. The quicker response of the engines was dumbed down by the computers to match jet fuel engines, yet that could be canceled in nanoseconds. The airline welcomed the experimental use of these planes, something prohibited with paying passengers. Usually, too, it was done by the research and development of the manufacturer, but with the enormous interests of the fossil fuel industry in aviation, the manufacturer couldn't take the chance to experiment with such equipment. On a smaller scale, and involving those who controlled politicians, government agencies, banks, and corporations directing exceptions and allowances, C-Know was able to use the planes. Besides, it made C-Know much more economical.

The planes were equipped with sufficient computers to include all the information of mankind's development; the steering committee deemed useful, should a small group of people survive a catastrophe that required mankind to start over. Instead of those who successfully were sheltered and survived continuing humanity as before, starting over from basic survival, the C-Know plan was to use airplanes to stay above the planet until they could reasonably return to the ground, especially airplanes not fuel dependent, so life could continue with information about everything useful.

The computers held no information about weaponry, about systems that didn't serve the common interests, about controls or exploitation, or about systems that created pollution when other technology could be used. Heirloom seeds of plants useful for foods and known medical benefits were stored in the planes. Life support supplies were carried to care for the people on board the plane until they could produce from their new land.

The planes themselves were entirely peaceful, having no weapon systems, defensive or offensive. To include weaponry was to risk passing even the idea of weapons to humanity after whatever calamity befell it.

There were four stations with duplicates of the same machines developed on the island for dissipating old energy bundles that distort emotion in the moment and negating programming and conditioning imposed on unsuspecting viewers and listeners through the media.

The cargo areas of the planes were used to create two levels, with a spiral staircase near the entry doors between the levels. Luxurious group and individual quarters were designed into the plane, as the uber-wealthy were frequent passengers. Those wealthy often developed their competencies in Sequoia's center and flew in the aircraft in the off-chance the flight they were on would be the one to survive following a catastrophe. In exchange for their resources and influence, the planes were designed to their comfort specifications. There was a small classroom for meetings, with twelve stations made with first class seating and the latest in interactive computer technology. Students could learn together or individually with three-dimensional holograms to explore and learn about their interests. With all the information in the computers, students could choose from among all the possibilities that were chosen for the future of mankind.

The lounge had a curious round sofa with a walkway through it and a round console in the middle, with a variety of functions for viewing outside the plane where the pilots couldn't see, a play station, or just for socializing.

The galley was anything but a place for airplane meals. It was equipped with space-age equipment for food preparation. Compact, lightweight kitchen gadgets seemed familiar yet looked strange. There was a big built-in refrigerator with an independent freezer. The refrigerator was stocked with fresh foods, organic and planned for optimum health. The pantry contained spices and dried foods. A professional chef was among the crew for every flight. The chefs too had developed their proficiencies and prepared food on the island.

The bathroom facilities were luxurious, with showers on the top floor and a water treatment system on the lower floor that returned all water to purified form.

C-Know members had airline crew identifications to enable them to come and go through security without unusual notice. The more famous among them wore uniforms and traveled as ordinary airline employees, as part of their practice of invisibility.

The flights usually held twenty to twenty-five people, including an essential crew of pilots, the control center operators, the chef, and a general manager to take care of essential needs on board. After completing competencies on the island, many of the people went through pilot training to the level of multi-engine ATPs, so they booked many hours flying C-Know planes, rotating with the pilots for the usually long flights. Although automation was generally superior to human abilities, these pilots had developed their competencies and had even greater capabilities. Piloting C-Know planes required readiness for what may never happen and the use of competencies for extraordinary piloting, should the extraordinary occur. That, in itself, was a discipline that stretched competencies to new levels of awareness. Simulations were created during flight in which the plane flew itself and created unusual scenarios for the pilots to respond to, including artificial visibility and sensory experience with instrument information supporting the simulations, all the while the plane flying safely and orderly per flight regulations.

There were always predictions that garnered sensationalism, excitement, and plenty of fear of the world being destroyed by an angry and vengeful god. They weren't the motivation of C-Know. Real possibilities from pressures of the earth's surface and the mystery of the molten core of the planet were possible. Collision with objects from space, electromagnetic shifts, or changes in the sun's supply of energy were possible. Governments or religions using weapons of mass destruction, it went without saying, were the most probable catastrophe.

As with so many good ideas, C-Know's project was motivated by theories. The usefulness of what they were doing had both here-and-now usefulness and a high probability of preserving the best of mankind's accomplishments, along with a few people to carry them forward. C-Know was already showing signs of disinterest, as the numbers of people taking the flights had been dwindling. If anything, being so intent, and spending so much time in aircraft just-in-case, had brought people to an awareness of how much they enjoyed everything in life available to them on the surface. The motive to survive past theories of mass destruction of property and life on earth was less attractive than taking the risk to enjoy every moment of life on the ground.

Still, C-Know was continuing as planned for the education of the young people, who could pursue any interest in depth, expanding their experience and having a true sense of being citizens of the planet. Language and cultures had real meaning to them, living all around the world, with people representing worldwide cultures, races, and economic status. They were always learning together, partying together, and being affectionate with each other, without inhibitions. The lifestyle carefully protected children and young adults from the fear, guilt, and shame messages and experiences usually associated with human sexual nature. There were rules about safe sex and knowing the difference between their lifestyles and those of the world around them, so they would know appropriate places to be themselves and not draw attention from those steeped in guilt, fear, and shame associated with sexuality. The planes, along with the ground communities and the space station being prepared to move out in space, were safe zones for all C-Know members to be themselves.

In the airport terminal, televisions were broadcasting CNN news. It had been updated to the Church News Network, as the American Parley presidency was well into its third year. His presidency had been continued indefinitely due to the declared moral emergency the church puppet government imposed. Only people who were interviewed and found living certain standards of "god's law" could vote.

The American Church had used its tithing money to become a financial empire. With returns on investments and ongoing member tithing, they methodically bought up companies that had influence on people, primarily the media and services that support the media.

The long-term goal was to place their priesthood representative in the White House and run the United States; the church presiding officer would tell the priesthood president, his staff, and other politicians (who were also supported through their system) what to do and when. For the president and staff, there was the assurance that everything they did would be directed by their god.

The Patriot Act had been made into a moral enforcer, giving police state authority to use any means they believed necessary to stop suspected immoral activities. People were disappearing without a trace, without the former constitutional rights, and yet the church and its government proclaimed the Constitution's original intentions were restored.

In the beginning of the Parley presidency, the maverick news agencies and underground news groups were silenced after revealing how Parley became president and the plan he was the faithful servant of. The news agencies and their people vanished, and then the church-owned and -operated news agencies debunked the reports and continued with the church-state propaganda.

While passing through the concourse, the group of six young people going to be on today's flight paused at one of the televisions. There was a public service announcement. With beautiful pictures, it started: "You are gifted with freedom of choice as your god-given birthright!" Then the scenes changed to disturbing scenes of people on drugs or with obvious diseases. "Wrong choices take away this special gift." Then the scene changed to prison work camps. "Make wrong choices and your choices are made for you." Next came the scene of a beautiful wedding, with the words "Chastity until one man and one woman marries."

Then the news resumed: "President Parley was somber today as he summed up the state of the world."

The scene flashed to the president at a podium, saying, "The world is in danger. God wants everyone to be obedient. Those who continue to resist rehabilitation are endangering all of us. God is losing patience. After the earth was cleansed with the great flood, god declared next time he destroyed the world, it would be with fire! I appeal to those of you holding out to come forward in repentance, unifying in god's will, and saving all of us from god's wrath."

Then the screen changed to another public service announcement: "If you know of anyone who is involved in sexual sins or immoral acts, particularly those known as LGBTQ, god will condemn you if you don't report them right away! Help them, help all of us, serve god, report now!"

The six young people were children of C-Know parents; Monique, thirteen, Casey, sixteen, Hiro, sixteen, Ersaline, fourteen, Jessica, seventeen, and Amandeep, fifteen, were on their way to their flight and knew they were under surveillance cameras; they couldn't show any signs of reaction to what they'd just seen. Their telepathic communication was instantaneous. Their choice was to become invisible or to act out roles that would appear acceptable. They'd played with theatre and had favorite scenarios they'd made up to display out in public. They leisurely walked toward the plane. They were in active conversation but without speaking, without language.

The moments watching the news caused them to evaluate what was going on in the United States, and thus imposed on the world, in contrast with all they'd been raised to know. It was a big difference to reconcile. For starters, they knew their lifestyle to be peaceful and loving; it opened them to gifts and abilities uncommon in human experience. They certainly weren't decadent and couldn't agree anything about them justified being called wrong in any way. Yet there were cunning forces of old energies, cleverly repeating the Inquisition.

They knew they had powers beyond what those burned at the stake had in their time. They knew they lived their sexuality beautifully and could see they were clearly different in beautiful ways because of the health of their sexuality. They could not understand the intensity of the opposite forces, the other side of the coin, which balanced the building energetic presence of their lifestyle. They knew not to call what balanced them evil and to give them as little energy as possible, avoiding any thoughts of challenging the right of the opposition to exist.

They knew a showdown between polar opposites was imminent. They weren't in the moments of showdown yet, but their wisdom was that the efforts of the church-state would generate its own counterbalance forces that would put them back in check. It wouldn't require members of C-Know do anything but to continue being themselves.

Sudheer was following the young C-Know members. He observed the energetic disturbance in them from pausing to watch the television. He sensed a need to coach the young people on today's flight in knowing enough to be aware but not getting caught up in it to the point fear would compromise each one of them and C-Know itself. He dreaded these times coming, perhaps because he sensed they would do just that.

Scera and Redbird were pilots for the flight. It had been a long time since they'd flown together, so there was a warm reunion between them. While Sequoia and Teuton were deeply involved as business partners, Teuton took time to be within the community, something Sequoia was insulated from. He'd taken many flights independent of her. They were always in communication, so physical distance wasn't a challenge. This would be the first time in nine months they'd taken a flight together.

Sudheer was there as learning coach for everyone, particularly the young people. It was customary for flight learning to begin with a discussion of the hot topics, to bring them to as much resolution or understanding as possible, to make it easier to focus on learning. Sudheer was preparing himself for what he was sure would be the hot topic for today with the six young people.

Taj, Elekcia, Viplow, Ashwini, Saladin, Jasmine, and Jaing joined the flight for a combination of continuing their education and rotating to another community on Madagascar.

Gabriel, a native from Mexico, was the flight engineer. He was twenty-eight years old, with a strong, athletic build. His black hair was well groomed. His brown eyes sparkled with the excitement his life of extreme sports and rare opportunities his alertness and quick actions had earned him. It was exactly his talent for watching in readiness to pounce on the moment at the first notice of need, for a shift in how an adventure was being played out, that brought him to the C-Know island experience. Gabriel knew the reason he was with C-Know was anticipation of the possibilities for adventure never before experienced by mankind. The whole idea of being the pivotal person to make intense choices for the preservation of mankind, for Gabriel, was worth the possibility that life would continue as it usually does.

Gabriel's job required him to survey the entire interior of the aircraft, mostly monitoring a room of computerized equipment only he was trained to thoroughly understand. He was required to be focused, alert, and attentive to multiple tasks, understanding how to interface and coordinate their use, as might be needed. He also knew his job had no precedent, so he must know his trade well enough to be able to use everything in the best possible way, when called upon to do so. Perhaps such ability will never be needed, but if and when it was, Gabriel must be ready to perform at a high level.

As he inspected the power-generating equipment, Teuton thought to himself, *When will people quit believing in that which makes them afraid, that which is sensational, that which titillates and engrosses them? All in all, someone profits, enjoying power and fame, while the followers, hungry for something sensational, give otherwise fools ... their fifteen minutes of fame.*

Can the planet once again become so volatile that fragile life forms like humanity will once again be unable to survive here?

Teuton paused ... aware of himself, his thoughts, the feelings driving them. Who was he trying to convince? Was he perhaps trying to convince himself of something, when he knew something else?

Saladin closed and secured the door for flight. The plane began to move. The screens that covered the walls above the sofa continued to show the entire scene around the airplane as it moved toward the taxiway. Planes were in various stages of landing, taxiing, and positioning for take-off. The passengers observing the screens around the round sofa felt like they were sitting on top of the plane. Even pilots don't see much through their windows; this room had a complete panorama view.

They were soon positioned on the runway, power applied to the engines; the plane quickly accelerated to the nose lifting and the airport disappearing below. Being in the front of the plane was usually quieter than behind the engines, but this airplane was unusually quiet.

While Gabriel would have readings from monitoring equipment throughout the plane, Saladin was checking all equipment to verify that electronic monitoring was operating correctly. The value of the contents of this plane couldn't be calculated, indeed to put out that information on any level, even with letters and memos within C-Know, could draw unwelcome attention. The value of the contents, if ever needed for what they might be needed, would be beyond estimation. No amount of precious metals and jewels could match the contents of this aircraft ... if ever needed.

Around the globe, six other planes were in various stages of flight or landing. They were strategically timed so three or more of the planes were always airborne. All of the planes carried the same cargo and equipment, all clones of one another. This was essential to C-Know's plan.

Scera had trained as a pilot, and her merits led to her being one of C-Know's most experienced pilots, a job that included being an instructor. Being gifted much like Sequoia, Scera helped pilots develop their flying skills with their proficiencies. C-Know pilots must be able to respond to a sudden moment's change from their moment's knowing.

They traveled eastward, according to their flight plan, to a higher than usual altitude, at which time they were cleared to turn northward to be above the east-west traffic of North America and overfly the polar ice cap on their flight to Madagascar.

CHAPTER 7

———⌇∿◦◦⌒◌⌒◌⌒◌⌒⌇∿◦◦∿———

Suddenly, everyone was startled, so startled their attention was totally grabbed away from whatever they were doing. Each person immediately started searching in bewilderment. Scera and Redbird searched the flight deck and the area visible to them outside the cockpit. Gabriel poured over his display screens. Taj, Elekcia, Jaing, Ashwini, Jasmine, and Viplow, sitting around the console, searched the video screen panorama for something. Sequoia had a far-away look in her eyes, shocked and pained.

After a while, Sequoia came back to the others, now each searching the eyes of one another, no one able to speak. Gabriel and Saladin were in their workstation. Whatever was going on was totally shared, so undeniably strong, all were experiencing it.

Those sitting around the sofa already had headphones on. Sequoia and Teuton joined them, reaching under the table-console to get headphones.

Elekcia was first to speak: "Okay, we all get there's something going on. Let's empty our minds of thoughts and discover what comes to us.

"Now, you guys up front, imagine you're in our circle, holding hands with us. All of you in the classroom, please come join us. Those of us back here will hold hands. Let's go into this together. Let's have this experience together. Something is going on in the Oneness we're part of. It isn't separate from us. Whatever is going on is part of us too."

Silence followed. Time became eternal.

From their C-Know island proficiencies, they all knew getting a psychic hit, getting a message, tuning into knowingness, receiving, is only hindered by and takes time to get past barriers of mind. When mind becomes silent, no time is required at all.

"Something is really strong in the dark side. Something is happening or about to happen," Scera said, breaking the silence.

Ashwini added, "What I am getting is inevitability ... something inevitable is happening we cannot reverse, something we've got to go with ... to accept. It is really dark, but I also get that darkness is acting strongly, and then there will be a shift to the light ... just as strongly. I don't want to go there specifically. We need to just witness it, be alert, and watch as it unfolds however it does. If we know all about it in advance, it will take us away from the moment-to-moment, living it in the now, and we'll have set our minds racing with it in advance, so we won't really be present to deal with it."

Viplow said, "Another way to say it is, don't worry right now, just be alert and watchful, and be ready for things as they happen. You'll do your best, dealing with it that way."

Jaing further explained, "If you are told only one part of it, you might get trapped in beliefs, and not be ready for everything else as more happens.

"We must be careful. If we want too much of a story right now and spend our time each contributing to making a story, things will continue to unfold rapidly, and we may miss a lot, and because we're missing making appropriate decisions in the moments as they happen, we might make a string of mistakes that lead to disaster."

"Since this is a round sofa, everyone spread around and watch the screen in front of you," Jasmine suggested. "And we should buckle our seatbelts again."

"Everything above us is on the ceiling monitors, but where is what is going on under us?" Viplow queried.

"Oh, switch off the console equipment you were using," Saladin said. "Now the table has a screen in it that displays what the bottom cameras are showing."

"That's mostly showing us what we can't do anything about," Viplow said, "but it still could give us important information."

Saladin asked, "What's going on in the flight deck?"

"We've been trying to pay attention to everything we can," Redbird said. "Most everything is normal, except there have been some bursts of static on the radio. Air Traffic Control has been quiet for a while, but the sun sometimes creates static, and there might not be much happening with flight following right now. However, they usually advise us of sun activity that may affect radio work."

"It's too soon to tell right now," Scera said. "It's still a wait-and-see situation. Keep helping us by watching the skyline on your monitors. You weren't told this before, but you're part of flying this plane. We need you to report what you're observing on your screens 'cause we don't have 'em."

"Are those the northern lights?" Ashwini asked.

"Where?" several asked at once.

"Right there," Ashwini exclaimed as she pointed. "Something happened, there was a bright flash, but it is gone now."

"Keep watching," Gabriel said. "Aurora Borealis usually is seen in low light and to the north. What direction were you looking, Ashwini?"

"Let's see, we're traveling north at 15 degrees right now," Scera said. "Where is Ashwini sitting?"

"I'm sitting at the rear of the port side of the couch, looking across," Ashwini reported.

"Then you're looking toward northeast. That's in our view too, but we might have been looking inside at the moment you saw whatever it was," Scera came back with.

"Where are we right now?" Teuton asked.

Gabriel replied, "We're headed north along the east side of the Rocky Mountains. We're over eastern New Mexico. To our east would be Amarillo, Texas. To our north is Denver. On the other side of the mountains to the west is Albuquerque. We can't see any of them right now.

"We're in a part of the continent where there is low population density; because of the curve of the earth, the dense population areas are out of our visual range."

"Hey, I just saw two flashes of light," Taj interjected. "They were a strange color but didn't last long enough to tell the rest of you to look."

"Where are you looking?" Scera asked.

"To the east," Sequoia replied. "I'm sitting on Ashwini's left. There went another one!"

"Wonder what they are?" Redbird said. "I'm watching to the east out the window ... hey, I just saw one too."

"Me too," several voices broadcasted at once.

"Oh crap," Scera burst out. "I just saw two flashes in front of us, and there appears to be something rolling toward us ... *Emergency!*"

Immediately a restraint system activated around the sofa, securing each person around their lower legs and chests with netting coming down to contain anything around the table that might be loose.

"Hold on!" Scera yelled.

A violent shock hit the plane, mostly head-on but also from beneath, shoving the plane up thousands of feet in altitude. There was a brief, deafening roar. Then another, less intense.

"Watch out to the east!" Scera called out.

She banked the plane sharply left, to the west, to be traveling as much as possible in the same direction of the next shock wave. The plane was overcome with shuddering and a deafening roar that seemed to kick the plane like a football and flip it into a barrel roll from the shock, hitting the broader surfaces of the wings from underneath as they pointed upward and downward in the turn.

Autopilot returned the plane to straight and level flight.

"Assess for damage," Gabriel ordered. "Heading 210 degrees immediately."

The emergency activated phase 2. Gabriel became commander of the flight. This was the kind of moment he was always on the alert for. He scanned his instruments, which were giving him information to help with this kind of event.

The plane climbed and then descended; the engines powered, there was a tilt starboard, then portside.

"Flight controls working," Redbird barked.

"Radio full of static ... some voices ... unintelligible," Scera reported.

"Navigation systems operational with GPS. Ground signals not operating," Gabriel said.

"We've got mushroom clouds rising in Colorado," Teuton reported.

"Oh god, not this," Scera replied in dread.

"Heading 165 degrees," Gabriel ordered. "We've got to avoid Albuquerque."

"The horizon isn't looking good to the east; don't know what to make of the colors in the sky," Elekcia reported.

No one seemed to notice Sequoia. She was sitting like a Buddha, with hands in a mudra position and eyes closed. She somehow had avoided the leg restraints.

"It's the atomic war scenario," Gabriel reported. "We anticipated shock waves. We've survived well so far. If we've got nuclear blasts going on, we've got to get away as fast as possible. Climb to the maximum altitude she'll fly, maintaining 600 knots.

"That's too close to the sound barrier!" Scera retorted.

"Get out of your training and into the moment," Gabriel ordered. "Saladin, what are the effects of nuclear explosions?"

"Well, there's an immediate flash of light that can evaporate life within a certain range of the ground zero," Saladin said. "Then a shock wave. Then an implosion of air rushing back to the point of explosion, which causes a cloud of dust, debris, moisture, and radiation to lift up into the sky, forming a mushroom cloud. The radiation affects energy, but what we've only theorized is how this might be for the more modern bombs, since they haven't been tested. We don't know what the effect of a mixture of types of bombs might be. Hell, what does it matter? We've got enough warheads on this planet to nuke all of life many times over."

"Radiation levels are getting higher. I think we better stay high, go fast, and head south. Maintain current altitude and 600 knots speed," Gabriel ordered. "Who would nuke countries in the southern hemisphere?" he uttered under his breath.

"Who is getting hit?" Scera shouted.

"I don't know," Gabriel said. "There's never news from a disaster area when the infrastructure is knocked out. The radio is just static. We have no contact with anyone. We're on our own right now. It's lucky all the plane's internal electronics are working right now."

"Who would do something like this?" Scera pleaded. "We didn't even have a warning. What's going on?"

"We may never know. This is suicidal lunacy," Taj muttered.

"Set the autopilot for Easter Island," ordered Gabriel.

Seconds turned into minutes, minutes to hours, as the small group waited, wondering what would happen next. Will it be a sudden spiraling, like the plane had just been released from the hand of a quarterback? Would there be more flashes of light? Everyone was securely strapped in. Holding hands was the only comfort available.

The younger people weren't accustomed to nuclear attack sirens and protocols experienced in the early years of the threat of nuclear war. Were they aware of the possibility of life suddenly ending without seeing something coming, without any warning more than what was already experienced?

What of El Paso, the last city in the United States they would fly near? Would El Paso explode with the blast the plane would not endure? There was no mushroom cloud in its direction.

Sequoia continued sitting still and silent in her meditation position.

Eyes were glued on the panorama screens.

Gabriel was intense under the weight of expectations placed on him to understand the data coming into his center, adding the human elements of sixth sense receiving, and knowing that made the difference between computers and the divinity of being human. There was no time to be distracted by fear or personal thoughts; he had to respond at his best at each moment. He realized the drama was taking him into his mind, and he needed to extend the time of being in moment, where he would know also witnessing the information at his station.

On the flight deck, Redbird monitored flight systems, alternating with watching the small amount of the world a pilot gets to see. Several aircraft were leaving contrails, all heading southbound also. The plane's radar would warn of other aircraft, but the most advanced form of warning was absent, the ground-based flight following of Air Traffic Control. With closing speeds of over a thousand miles per hour, by the time a plane traveling northward was recognized, it would be all but impossible to take evasive action. Yet with a big sky, occupying the same space at the same moment, away from airport traffic, wasn't so much of a concern to him.

A timer beeped every two minutes, alerting Redbird and Scera to switch from looking outward to focus within the flight deck, alternating so one of them was always watching the sky.

Saladin worked the radios, scanning frequencies for human contact. Static and radio interference filled her ears. Never before had she been in a plane without outside contact. Normally, the left seat was the designated pilot-in-command, and the final command of the flight controls were the captain's, but the command of the mission was now transferred to Gabriel as stage 2 was activated. The aircraft's intercom system continued to work well. The aircraft itself was fortified with all known electrical and electronic protections. What was beyond their control was everything else outside the aircraft's skin.

Indeed, the plane's inhabitants were without information, only being able to deduct from a brief handful of observations what was happening. This aircraft had the best equipment possible to detect and deal with calamities, but now, it seemed small by comparison to the forces that appeared to have been unleashed.

"Gabriel, do you have our position?" Sudheer asked.

"We're over northern Mexico," he reported, "192 miles south of the New Mexico border."

Sudheer sighed in relief. If anything happened in El Paso, it wouldn't affect them now.

"Satellite signals for GPS are still working," Gabriel said, "but there's a lot of distortion; the computers are still sorting out the information well enough for our guidance system. Otherwise, all we have is the onboard equipment for information. Keep scanning your panorama screens and report anything unusual. I have the same screens reduced on my station monitor, but I can't see much ... each picture is way too small."

"Can you make any more of the situation?" Sudheer asked Saladin.

"The horizon behind us shows mushroom clouds spreading out," she said. "Looks like St. Elmo's fire across the sky, amazing hues in indigo, near the end of the spectrum of visible colors."

"What about ahead of us? What about Mexico's cities?" Jasmine asked.

"Mexico's constitution prohibits war outside its borders," Gabriel replied. "They're not a threat to anyone."

"Well, whoever did this isn't leaving Mexico undisturbed. It doesn't look too good out toward its populated areas," Scera exclaimed.

Gabriel ordered, "Autopilot off. Heading 225 degrees. We've got to get over the Pacific Ocean."

"What are the sensors picking up?" Viplow asked.

"Some pretty amazing stuff," Gabriel replied. "Problem is, the computer wasn't programmed with experience, because testing stopped before technology developed to sense what we can sense now. The information is recording. That's all. Just not enough information, and it doesn't match with anything in the computers to say what it is, or give scenarios to work with. There was little information to enter into the computers for a nuclear scenario."

Sudheer decided to take a chance. He unbuckled his seatbelts, made his way to the staircase, and went to the upper floor, to the flight engineer's workstation. Gabriel was busy with his equipment, so Sudheer touched him on the shoulder to get his attention.

"Hey Gabby, I'm trying to remember information about aboveground nuclear testing. Too much is theory, because much has been developed after testing was halted, and there was never more than one device detonated at a time. We know radiation is carried in the weather patterns, and we know the radiation isotopes take different amounts of time to decay. We've heard there are enough warheads to destroy this planet several times over. What do you think?" Sudheer asked.

"We're to survive against all odds," he said. "I've been looking up information on nuclear accidents and what little was measured near aboveground nuclear testing. Containment is key in accidents, but once nuclear fallout escapes, it is not containable. A bomb is pure uncontainable radiation being blown right up into the atmosphere. I've chosen to go toward Easter Island for now. They're small and so isolated they might be forgotten by whoever is bombing. Almost all countries with nuclear warheads and all logistical targets are in the Northern Hemisphere. Our best chance for avoiding the first nuclear problems is going south. Global weather tend not to mix air from the Northern and Southern hemispheres very fast, so the radiation won't spread south as fast as it will spread around the Northern Hemisphere. We might have time in the south."

"I agree with that. Good thinking. Have you found out the critical mass of these nuclear explosions? What will that mean?" Sudheer inquired.

"It's all theory, like I said, but it suggests that since everything is made up of energy, and there's an interconnectedness to everything, there's a point at which the disturbance, the instability of hyperactive atomic material, will set all other energy into instability, and all matter will cease to have form. Or another way to put it is, all matter will change to a gaseous state. Earth would essentially be a star at that point."

"So if that's the case," Sudheer said thoughtfully, "we're near to being a scientific experiment of whether that theory is correct, and if it is, we'll cease to be … everything will cease to be, and possibly even our energetic essence will be disturbed or mutated."

"Yeah, but we've got to put all we can into surviving and solving problems, as long as we aren't obliterated," Gabriel reiterated. "We might cease to be any moment, but remember, at that moment, we must be giving our all to help humanity survive. We're the key to humanity's future on this planet."

"Okay, we've got to have a discussion," Sudheer said. "We've got to be honest with each other for sure but also allay the fears the flight/fight/freeze response is naturally causing. I just want to be sure we're on the same page. Thanks. I'm going to get everyone on the intercom."

Sudheer carefully found his way back to his seat in the classroom and once again put on his headphones.

Teuton noticed Sequoia was continuing to sit in a lotus posture. He knew she was holding a space for everyone and helping those on board the plane to be protected. It also involved shielding the group from the unprecedented intense shock and bewilderment of massive death, of people assessing their status and beginning to understand what to do once they've figured out they're no longer in an earthly body.

After putting on his headphones, Sudheer spoke on the intercom: "Okay everyone, listen up. We're all in our own thoughts and wondering a lot of things right now. There's a lot going on, and we've got to decide what is going on with us.

"We know very little. Communication with the world outside this plane is out. We're safe right now. We're the luckiest people right now, because we've got the best of the best on this plane, and that means the best chance to survive we could possibly have.

"Let's get real. We all know what mushroom clouds at the center of blasts and flashes of light are about. I think we've got to address our fears of a nuclear war going on. We're thinking about it, anyway."

"Are we going to die from what's going on?" Jasmine asked.

"It's too soon to tell," Sequoia said, suddenly speaking up.

"Well, when will we know?" Jaing pleaded.

"This plane was designed to survive. It's loaded with the most valuable information and technology known to mankind," Sequoia answered for everyone to hear.

"Our mission is to survive anything and use all our resources to enable mankind to recover," Elekcia added.

"Well, that's nice for us," Scera said, "but what about everyone down there? What about our loved ones?"

Sequoia said, "Some things we don't have answers for. Some things we just cannot do anything about. I'm really sorry. You must feel really shocked and sad. I think we all do. Gabriel, can we take off these seat restraints so we can hold and comfort each other?"

"Go ahead," he said. "Need overrides protocol."

Everyone unbuckled and retracted their seat restraints. Sequoia made her way around to being the group hug. She became intently aware that with the risk of everyone being evaporated with critical mass being reached, human contact and comfort became the most important thing. It felt good to be holding Teuton with the others. She realized how little they'd touched. She began to see folly in her position with him. Was she really beyond sex? She didn't want to think the obvious, but it was there. She regretted she hadn't been intimate with Teuton and realized she might not get the chance the rest of her life, which might end any moment.

Vulnerability was more and more alive in her. She thought about her status as uber-wealthy and privileged; the guru leader for higher consciousness in her was replaced by the equality of facing a sudden death. She knew it was possible that nearly everyone in her world, everyone she'd interacted with in life, was already dead, having experienced extreme forces jamming them out of their bodies, possibly even vaporizing them with intense heat. The thoughts took her into suffering she'd never known, where she couldn't remember what to do, although she usually coached others in what to do to get through suffering. She didn't know which would consume her first: her deep despair of feeling in the universal consciousness or her inner vulnerability.

She squeezed his body a little more. She loved him. She always loved him. Why did she insist he prove his love to her by not being complete in it? Why did she play what now seemed a game, as if life would always be the same and she could change her mind any time it suited her? Now she may end this lifetime with a best friend and lover she played the guru with, and now with this shock, she realized her guru thing wasn't true. She couldn't find the moment. Her thoughts raced with stories and scenarios that were probably true, and she was overcome with the energy of despair, pain, grief, and shock of possibly billions of people being forced out of their incarnations. Their turn may come in a moment. She felt everyone squeezing even tighter.

Teuton felt Sequoia's hand tightening on his waist and being pulled even tighter against her. His heart was so filled with sadness, and he was comforted by the female touch of his beloved. He knew he knew what to do to get through everything, but the weight of all that was happening felt like more than he could overcome. He wasn't even sure he wanted to live through something when everyone else would probably not survive. It was his life story to survive what others didn't. All the competencies were hanging in a balance, with the other side being whether Teuton had the will to choose his competency over giving up in the massive despondency of massive death of the worst kind, the few killing the many.

Still, he felt the warmth and love in the group and had his arm around, right or wrong, the one person he would live through anything to continue with. Something was incomplete, but he'd successfully put the possibility of sexual communion with Sequoia out of the realm of possibility, so he only felt the emptiness without any explanation.

Time sped up for those comforting themselves, yet for Gabriel and the pilots, it continued to go in slow motion. Being all alone with their thoughts when they wanted so much for something else to be the case, to be happening all the while in a soup of despondency and despair was consuming them too. For those embracing each other, there was temporary reprieve, to be touching, being touched, and embracing, feeling perhaps for the first time just how powerfully soothing an embrace was.

"We are living," Sequoia told the group. "We're on a mission to live. It's very important, and each one of us is essential. Don't let your thoughts be about dying. Let your thoughts be about living, wondering what new things you're going to be doing. This plane is about human survival in the best ways possible, and because you're here, you're important. It's all right to mourn for those who have left their bodies, for whom this lifetime has ended. They'll be counting on you to do what they would do if they were with you right now. There are a lot of beings available to guide and help each of us now.

"I've got the perfect idea," Sequoia proclaimed in a hopeful tone. "Let's go into the sleeping quarters, set up a massage table, and work on each other. I'll bet we all could benefit from a massage and some energy work to calm us down and help us to think clearly."

With that suggestion, those at the tables and in the classroom got up and went into the sleeping quarters.

Teuton and Elekcia took a shift at the aircraft's controls, giving Scera and Redbird some time to rest and rejuvenate while participating in the massage and energy work.

Redbird said, "While we're still on the intercom together, I'd like to talk about something for a few minutes if we can. I've been thinking about all the death and destruction that must be behind us. There's a lot of people I care about who are probably dead or suffering right now. I don't know why I have a right to live on without injury when people I love have been devastated.

"I've also been thinking of how we might die. The radiation could hit critical mass, and I guess that wouldn't be too bad, because death would be instant. The plane could fall to pieces in the sky. We've got to land sometime, and we may be injured or die in a crash. If we do happen to land safely, then we may eventually suffer and die from radiation sickness."

Gabriel added, "Yeah, I've been thinking about these things, too. Maybe those who died quickly were the lucky ones. Maybe the joke is on us. Thinking we are going to survive, we may have actually preserved ourselves for the worst fate of all."

"Who was so crazy to think they had a right to end life on this planet?" Ashwini asked. "And now I'm scared. Maybe they died before they knew they were going to die. Now we know were going to die and it might be really painful."

As it seemed like the tears and pain were lessening, Redbird spoke with bitter anger: "Whoever did this is the most evil monster in the universe. Everyone loses. Just because they wanted to die, they didn't have the right to take everyone else out with them. Who thought they had that right? Look what we have to go through because of them. Look what everyone has to go through because of them. And there's nothing I can wish on them, because they already blew themselves to bits, or if they're still alive, they'll die from the radiation. I can't believe it's finally happening. May they roast forever in a pit of radioactive waste … the bastards!"

"It's that damned church," Jaing blurted out. "They've created Armageddon. They make up their god and then project their insanity into the god they create. Then they believe their god tells them to do things for him. They're probably sitting smugly in shelters, thinking this is god's moment."

Scera burst out, "Okay, I just don't want to deal with this. There's no use thinking about this stuff. We can't do anything to change what's happened. Just leave it alone and do our jobs."

With that, Sequoia decided to give some direction to the energies among them. With a motion, she directed Redbird to lie on one of the massage tables.

Scera first did a series of movements on Redbird's back to calm his fight/flight/freeze reactions.

She directed Alekcia and Gaia to move to each side of Redbird, where they held his triple warmer sedating points. Then she instructed Gabriel to hold Redbird's feet, placing pressure on his shock points. Then Sequoia started doing energy work on Redbird's head. Scera began testing his flows of energy, treating those in need of adjustment.

Next, it was Gabriel's turn on the table, and when he was finished, they worked on everyone else, concluding with sessions for Scera and finally Sequoia.

Sequoia opened her eyes as she lay on the table. "You know, I still feel deeply for all the losses. I am still aware of what we're facing ahead of us, but I feel a lot different now. What about you?"

Redbird was first to reply: "I'm still indignant about what's going on. I really want to protest in any way I can, but I don't feel like fighting in a big explosion of rage."

Scera added, "Well, I feel like I can deal with it. I just wanted to run and hide, but there's nowhere to go."

Gabriel asked of Sequoia, "Did the angels teach you these techniques?"

At that question, Scera, Redbird, and all of the youth just stared at him.

Sequoia ventured an answer: "First of all, no, the angels didn't teach us these techniques. They're very ancient medical practices, combined with some modern insights. It's just energy medicine.

"As far as angels are concerned, I guess if you want to use that term, 'angel,' to talk about them …

Jaing couldn't hold back: "What are you talking about? I thought those things were just a myth."

All of a sudden, a little old man in a wizard's cape appeared between the massage tables. "Well, right you are!" he said.

Everyone stepped back, with eyes as big as saucers. Redbird jumped back. The old wizard just laughed.

Then a younger woman's voice said, "We thought if we let you know we're here with you and gave you a good idea of who we are and what we are like, you would know the team you're working with a little better."

Everyone turned to see a middle-aged African woman standing near them. She continued, "You'll probably learn a lot more about angels by meeting us than trying to get an explanation from someone."

The old wizard said, "Don't believe what you see right here. And don't believe anything you've ever been told about those of us who are not in bodies. Through the ages, there's been a lot of different names for us. As mankind has told and retold the stories, the legends are much bigger than life. Besides, what was left out of the stories was who really had the power, and who were the helpers?"

The woman added, "We can take any form we want to, to be visible to you. Next time you see us, you will be looking at another form, but you will know it is still us. So about these angels. That's a really old legend that started from people who saw helpers appearing, floating in the air, who really didn't know how to explain it to other people. So they created the idea of people with wings, and somehow the name 'angel' got attached to that. So for people who believe in that idea of angels, it's easiest to appear before them with wings. They don't get so frightened, and for them, it's a sign that the visitor comes representing the highest. It's something that works, but it also creates some confusion."

The old wizard said, "You must know very clearly just how powerful you are. We can't be letting you think we are the beings of legend. You have got to be in your own power, and you've got to know that we are simply your helpers. You make the decisions, you do the asking, and when you're very clear about what you're asking for, it's easy for us to help you.

"There are times you won't have time to ask somebody else what to do. If we appear to you in the legendary forms, and you think that we are the ones who have to make the decisions and tell you the right way to go, that could make all the difference between success and failure of your mission. Things are just going to happen too fast to seek direction outside of yourselves. We'll do our part, but we are not the authority, and we are not going to be taking your power away from you.

"You don't have time for dowsing tools, you don't have time for spells and incantations, and you don't have time to do some ritual to make the magical and mysterious happen. You've just got to get on with it. I thought it might help for a wizard to tell you, you don't need to be encumbered by a wizard's tools."

The woman interjected, "He's not saying it all has to come from you. What he's saying is that you are the receiver. As the receiver, you take in all the information available in the moment, including telepathic input. Then you decide what to do with it, what help to ask for, and with your physical strength of being in a body, you intend, and energy accommodates. The more of you who work together with the same intention, the more clearly energy gets the instruction to accommodate. And we will help you with that.

"You don't have to take time to formulate words, even in your mind, to ask us. You don't have to formulate words in your mind to direct energy. As soon as you have the inception, you have broadcast what is necessary for us to help you and for energy to accommodate."

The wizard quickly added, "So that's just about as close to instant as can be. It isn't even necessary to formulate words in your mind. The inception thought that makes the difference preceded the words already. And you're doing that will make things happen, because formulating the words in your mind only detracts from the purity and strength of your creative thought.

"It took time for you to learn language, but you started with just pure thought. Remember, you thought before you could speak about what you thought."

Ashwini asked, "What are we supposed to do?"

The woman said, "You are a good example, Ashwini. You always need to be in a state of questioning. That keeps your channels open to taking in information. That's another reason the inception thought is so effective in its instant purity. Your energies need to be back to questioning and receiving. Once the decision is made, adding any ritual only spends precious time and takes energy away from questioning and receiving. In between, you decide what you are receiving, and you make a choice. I want you to know that you are always directing energy, and energy is accommodating you. You would have known that all your life if your thoughts were not so scattered and troubled."

The plane shook violently, and the people in bodies were thrown around the room. Then normal flight resumed.

Checking in with each other, everyone was well enough off. No one needed first aid. They returned to the visitors, more intent than ever to learn whatever they had to offer.

Scera wondered why they made such a big deal about defining themselves. She didn't care as long as they were helping. "What about all the people who are dead and suffering? Who is helping them?"

"There are more beings who are not in body, ready to help you, than you can possibly imagine. And don't worry about those who recently left their bodies; they are really concerned about you and ready to be focused to help you with what you need to be doing as you carry out your mission. Nobody ceased to be. They only changed their form, their energetic expression. They are more present and with you than they were when they were in bodies. Bring your energies back to loving them, to feeling connected with them, and to giving them the information they need to be of assistance to you."

The old wizard said, "You might think of yourselves as kings and queens, and they are your subjects, eager to carry out your wisdom."

The third voice spoke from a body that looked like a woman of the Amazon Basin. She said, "Gabriel, you've made a good choice to go south. After you've cleared populated areas of Central America, go Eastward over the Amazon basin of Northern Brazil. In Brazil, you will join with people who have been doing research and developing methods for preventing problems from radiation. It's been very secretive. In the wrong hands, the information would help destructive and evil people to use atomic weapons while protecting themselves. If they thought they could do that, without paying the price themselves, they would do the most vile crimes against nature that have ever been done. As you know so far, no one can use nuclear weapons on someone else and not also use them on themselves, and that has been what has prevented nuclear war until now.

"Religious megalomaniacs have set off the nuclear arsenals."

"We want you to know," the old wizard said, "there still is the possibility of surviving this holocost; humanity may continue better than before."

The African woman said in conclusion, "You will find answers within you." Then they all vanished.

Gabriel called everyone to meet in the classroom. Teuton remained in the pilot seat to monitor the aircraft. To include him in the meeting, everyone wore their headsets on the intercom system.

"I have done some research in the data system on nuclear fallout," Gabriel began. "After the bombing of Hiroshima and Nagasaki, as you know, many people died from radiation. What is little known is that the radiation did not affect some people. It was determined that the difference between those who were affected and those who were not had to do with diet. The people who are not affected ate significant amounts of seaweed. The unique contents of the seaweed somehow counteracted the effects of radiation.

"Because of the protection the seaweed diet gave, potassium iodide tablets were developed for people working in the nuclear industries, but they are not available to the general population.

"So what ideas have you thought of?" he asked, looking around the classroom.

Viplow spoke up: "Well, if everything is energy and radiation is just a hyper form of energy, and if we have the power to command energy, and we were in on the creation as we know it, then we must be able to somehow command the radioactive energy to change."

"What we need to do," Redbird suggested, "is either speed up the decay process of the radiation or to transmute it, transform it into something else that is either neutral or beneficial to the planet. Because there are different possibilities of what we can do with the radiation, it's important that we are all putting energy into doing the same thing. What I'm saying is that if we decide to put our energy into speeding up the decaying process, for instance, for the half-life of one isotope of radiation to change from twelve days to just a second, then we all put our creative energy into that. If we all decide to transmute the radiation into something beneficial, then we all do that. That way, our energies are not scattered, and we have a clear focus on commanding energy with congruence."

Jaing volunteered, "Another option would be to stop anything from being affected from radiation. We know from atomic structure that everything is energy, and the distance between each part of an atom is enormous. What quantum research has been trying to come to understand is how or why there can be anything solid, dense. It has been surmised that all of creation as we know it, as we experience it, is an illusion we created so we could have these experiences in bodies with the material world. So maybe it's all about the creation, design. If we created in the design that some forms of radiation would be more than living things could tolerate, we created the parameters of reaction of the material illusion to the intense energy of radiation. So if we created it that way, we can change the parameters of the creation, so the radiation won't affect life by the same rules it has in the past."

Elekcia added, "So we believe radiation will cause radiation sickness, harming plants and animals and the environment, and we observe it doing that, because we created it that way. So also because we observe that happening, we believe this is cause and effect, what must happen always. However, the information that Gabriel came up with about radiation and people who eat seaweed shows us that the effects of radiation do not follow ironclad rules."

Sequoia expressed her thought: "Another way to think of it is that we created the parameters the way they appear to be most of the time; we observe what we created, and we believe what we observe. The short version is, we created it, and we believe it. Isn't that exactly what we do all of time as we live our lives? We create our reality, and we believe the reality we've created to be real, and most often, we believe it comes from somewhere else, not us. So as it is on the small level of one individual, it is also on the grand level of our group reality. Neither one of them are really founded in scientific evidence, they just appear in the way we've created them. Energy is very compliant with us, even creating holograms or illusions because our thoughts or our intentions organize energy to create appearances."

Gabriel summarized, "So now what we need to do is to decide on the way we want energy to act. We can change the rules of the creation we made, which are not ironclad, we can change the nature of radiation, or we can just have the radiation dissipate in a hurry. I wonder what else we could do with it. For instance, could we have all excessive radiation just lift off into space, say, being attracted to the sun? Do we need the energy of radiation from nuclear warheads to stay on the planet?"

Saladin spoke next: "We could do that or just about anything else that we decide. The important thing is that we all be commanding the energy with the same intention, so we don't create confusion for energy and then nothing changes. We could just have the intention that all the radiation float up into the sky out of our atmosphere and keep on going toward the sun. We can make it as complicated as we want, or we can make it as simple as we want, as long as we do it together with unity of intention and method. It will happen."

Ashwini said, "Okay, I get what you're all saying, and I see some things we're going to have to deal with. First of all, we tell the helpers who are not in bodies what we want them to help us with, so they will be on the same page with us. Second, we don't know who else is still alive. Its possible billions of people are still alive. We're probably not going to be able to communicate with them to get them in agreement and on the same page with us. If they are in a state of panic, fear, or dread from their beliefs about what radiation is going to do to them, energy is not going to get a clear message to know what to do."

Sudheer said, "It isn't for us to take all the responsibility for doing this right now. When we land, wherever we decide to land, serendipity is going to gather us with like-minded people to add to our strength. Right now, since it has been decided to go to Brazil, and we know there's already a group with consciousness to stop radiation, we will do well to see if serendipity unites us with their project, so we can be on the same page with them.

"We can intuit what they're doing too and join them. Eventually, we need to get everyone doing the same thing. Well ... that's not likely, so another thing we can do is get on the same wavelength with as many people as possible, and those who cannot, for whatever reason, we need to energetically isolate … put them inside a protective bubble, so they don't confuse what we're doing. Remember, we have all the disembodied helpers that will focus their intent and creative energy with us when we're ready to do it."

Redbird reflected, "It seems a little strange to me after being taught all my life, and everyone around me believing, we have to placate and appeal to an external god to do things. My inner truth now, for the first time, knows that the strength of god comes from how much we join together with a singleness of intention; this is a huge shift. Do you think we are going to have to struggle with people's beliefs that all of the power comes from their gods and their angels, and their saints, and so on? Nobody's ever been able to get people to unite with a clear knowing of a deity and what divine power is. It's always been the biggest conflict on the planet.

"I am thinking about all of the people who just became disembodied and might be confused about where they are what happened, and what is going on for them now. Aren't they going to be loaded with the same beliefs they had before they transitioned?"

Sudheer replied, "Okay, I understand your concern. When people are in a state of fear, panic, and disarray, they put out a lot of confusion; scattered energy, but it has a very low impact upon energy. The more conscious people are, the more clear they are within, and the more they are able to focus their energy, the more they can create, the more they can contribute to group creation. Each person who is clear and conscious is easily 10,000 times more powerful than someone who is in unconsciousness.

"But it is better to neutralize them and contained whatever energy they are putting out so it doesn't affect the energy in a way that reduces the effectiveness of what we are doing. It only takes a moment to cause energy to shield and contain nonbeneficial energy."

Redbird continued, "It's still strange to me that with eons of people praying, with very little effectiveness, you're talking about us being able to do what we always wanted god to do. I am still unclear about where god is in this picture."

Elekcia answered, "Yeah, the religionists way back in history removed an essential part of the understanding of god. For one thing, by isolating god as a separate entity and the only entity with power, mankind could be exploited by the clever. I have never believed for a moment that sincere people who've gone into the priesthood ever knew that. It was just part of their teaching of what god is from early historic writings. Now we've got to come back to the basics. Godliness is within everything, and everything makes up the totality of god. We always had the ability to direct energy, to create. Groups who are focused together experience results and have been taught to praise god as an individual, separate entity for listening to them and granting their requests. People have been taught that whatever happens as what they would call an answer to prayer, has nothing to do with them personally, beyond their appealing to god. I don't think anybody has a problem believing that the love of god is something any of us can participate in. When it comes to the power of god, the concepts of blasphemy and heresy are built-in barriers, deterrents, to people exploring and learning about how they are an inseparable part of the power usually attributed to god."

Even deeper in contemplation, Redbird continued, "We've got to be accurate now. Need is too much, and we've got to be effective. The wake-up call is now."

Gabriel directed the meeting again: "Okay, the things we've been talking about, do they resonate with everyone's inner truth?"

Everyone gave a verbal response in the affirmative. There were no indications of anything contrary.

Gabriel said, "Then we will continue on to Brazil, asking for guidance to join us with those who've been working on dealing with the radiation of atomic explosions and nuclear waste. We've been talking about our roles as part of god and the active sense, in the yang energy. Let us not forget to be balanced yin energy, that of being silent and receptive, so that what needs to come to us gets through. We are passing west of Central America soon, so we need to be in tune with guidance for what to do now. So together we ask for that guidance, and then together we become silent and receptive so we can receive it effectively.

"Everyone good with that?"

All of the heads nodded in the affirmative. Teuton's voice came through the intercom: "I'm in."

CHAPTER 8

—⁓⦵⌇⌇⦵⌇⌇⦵⌇⌇⁓—

Teuton observed Sequoia was unusually occupied with something.

"Hey, amiga, what's going on?" Teuton asked. "You feeling okay?"

She replied, "Yeah, I've been getting some hits. The same thing happened when I was in high school. It's a strange feeling, pretty hard to describe unless you've experienced it too. I had almost forgotten all about it."

Teuton offered, "So give me a try, amiga. What are best friends for?"

She replied, "Okay. Here goes: I would have something that seemed to want to overtake me. I resisted a few times, insisting I stay in control of myself. Finally, one night in my dorm, the sensation came stronger than ever. Since my friends were there, I wasn't so afraid, so I just let it happen.

"As I surrendered myself into the experience, a voice began speaking with my body, but it wasn't my voice. Everyone thought I was kidding around.

"I guess I was asleep or something. My friends told me all about it, after it was over. We were frightened but excited about it all the same. Whoever was talking through my body told my friends things about themselves no one would know. It also told them some believable things about what was going on and gave them advice.

"We would do that as regular entertainment for get-togethers. For a while, it was quite a novelty. Then talk about it brought some problems. Parents got all upset, and I was called into the dean's office about it. Certain friends wouldn't have anything to do with me anymore, and some students started making fun of me.

"So I stopped."

Teuton sympathized, "Wow, that's a high price to pay for exploring the paranormal. I'm sorry you had to go through that, amiga."

In deep thought, she responded, "Yeah, it really hurt, and it continued. When I went to my five-year reunion, I was mocked by a couple of guys. People really act badly about what they don't understand, or are not allowed to accept, because of their belief systems.

"I'm a little afraid right now, amigo. I need you to stay with me on something, okay?"

"Sure," Teuton reassured her. "Is it happening again, now?"

"Yeah," she said, with trepidation in her voice.

Sensing her vulnerability, Teuton encouraged her: "Amiga, do you need to explore this again in a safe environment?"

"Yeah, that's what I need," Sequoia relented. "If there's anyone in the whole world that gets me, it's you, amigo. I need your support right now."

"Okay, what do we need to do?" Teuton asked.

Sequoia explained her predicament: "I feel that same kind of thing going on, like someone is knocking, wanting the door opened.

"I want to let it happen," she told him, "with you there to keep me safe."

Teuton expressed his understanding: "Amiga, I've used hypnosis to explore the paranormal. Let's see what it's about. Do you need to go into a deeply relaxed state, meditation, self-hypnosis, or shall I help you go into hypnosis?"

"*Muchas gracias, mi amigo,*" Sequoia replied. "Let's slip past everyone into the sleeping quarters. I'll go into a deep state of relaxation and let it happen. You listen and dialogue with me … whatever happens."

Teuton motioned for her to take the lead to the stairway; they descended and made their way to the sleeping quarters.

Once inside, Sequoia took a meditation position on her bed, and Teuton sat cross-legged in front of her. She started breathing long, deep breaths; after a couple of minutes, they slowed, followed by a big breath. A voice began speaking through her.

"I am the almighty creator of earth, conqueror of the galaxy. My name is Allah, my name is Vishnu, my name is Elohim. I am the Source. Whoever speaks my name, invokes my power. I Am from the beginning and continue until the end.

"All power for everything is from me. There is nothing created but by me. All is mine, for I have created it for my pleasure.

"You displease me, for you have forgotten the true religion. You have forgotten to praise, worship, and adore me for all I have done for you, and all I might do for you.

"You dare to undertake this mission without thinking of me, without asking me to make your mission a success, without paying homage to me for my favor.

"I command you to include all I am to tell you about my true religion, in what is in this, my aircraft. My truth has been lost again and again by mankind. I will restore it through you, my servants. I give you the privilege and honor to be the vessels through which I will restore the truth to mankind. I will give you the keys, make you the keepers of my holiest of secrets, and initiate you into the priesthood of privilege and power. You will learn the proper ways to appease me for my grace.

"First of all, I command all aboard this plane to come listen to me."

Obediently, Teuton got off the bed and extended his hand to Sequoia's body to help her follow him to the classroom. She was in a trance, her body sluggish and awkward. He gently assisted her to the classroom and then left to tell the pilots and Gabriel to come join him.

All gathered into the classroom and sat facing Sequoia.

"Well done, my good and obedient servants."

"What is this?" Scera asked.

From Sequoia's body, the deeply male voice penetrated with absolute authority:

"I am the one you call god, the Source of all there is."

"Are you going to fly this plane?" Scera interrupted.

"You fail to understand who I am …"

"And you fail to understand flying without ground support," Scera insisted, refusing to be intimidated.

"You will obey me," the voice ordered. "The consequence of displeasing me is eternal suffering."

"I am responsible for the safety of this flight," Scera said, "and any other aircraft we might need to avoid. I am going back to my duty station." She then got up and left.

An eerie silence followed. The others wondered if the channeling session was over.

With an even more commanding presence, the voice began speaking again: "Who is this defiant, insolent woman? A woman's place in the universe is subservient to the power and authority of the men who love me.

"This woman through whom I am speaking, Sequoia, is one of the most privileged and chosen women of all, for she is my vessel. Her celibacy has prepared her, purifying her, to serve me. Her sins are forgiven. She shall have no other man, for she is my bride.

Teuton said, "Excuse me, but the woman you called defiant and insolent is living her sense of duty and devotion; this is her highest calling when she is in a position of responsibility. Even you can understand and value that. I am certain that you value her loyalty."

"Yes, these are the qualities of a good servant," the voice said. "I have caused Armageddon to begin. I destroyed with water, now I destroy with fire! This planet is being cleansed of the scourge of disobedient creations who displease me. Because of your preparedness, I shall ensure you survive to help establish a new humanity, a humanity that fears me, that worships me, that obeys me, that will prosper and flourish with my blessings.

"I am the light of the universe. Without me, all would be in darkness. I love those who love me, and I destroy those who do not obey me. For those to whom I give much, much is expected. Much is expected of you.

"Now you will listen to instructions of he who serves on my right hand, who sits beside me at my throne, where legions of angels sing praises to me, where all adore me and know I am their source.

"Now listen to my faithful ruler of the Milky Way."

With that, a different voice spoke through Sequoia, another commanding male voice: "I am Shaweah, the divine president of the

Galactic Council of the Milky Way. The cleansing of earth is taking place. It will be a great celebration throughout the galaxy, as this planet is the most disobedient, the most defiant, and the most decadent planet in the Milky Way. The dark angel has successfully reaped countless souls from those who were placed upon this planet. He is getting his final harvest of souls. Those of you on this plane will not be among them."

Shaweah continued, "The purpose of any lifetime on this planet is obedience."

Teuton interrupted, "Obedience to what?"

"Obedience to the laws and commandments of the true religion. We are here to give you the true religion.

"The Source creates everything. His creations must honor him, must praise him, must worship him, and must serve him above all other interests.

"However, because you did not have the truth to guide you, and the intentions of your hearts were pure, you are being taught correctly, so you may repent and be forgiven. You are the elite of the Source, you are the chosen. There will be some who will survive the coming calamities of Armageddon. You will restore the true religion among them.

"These are your instructions:

"The best tool to keep his subjects in a state of acknowledging him is difficulty, misery, and most of all, fear. These are the keys to the priesthood.

"When people are fulfilled and happy, living without regard to the past or the future, they forget their creator. Therefore, they must constantly be prodded with reasons to be fearful, to be insecure about their state of being on earth. All of the stories that create fear are truths, because they turn people to their creator. The end justifies the means. If it turns people to worship the Source, he will be pleased, and all will receive of his blessings.

"When people are suffering, lonely, and destitute, give them the promise of constant overflowing love from the Source, in exchange for their obedience. When people are in a state of prosperity, they must be threatened with great loss to keep them obedient.

"When mankind believes in himself, when someone turns to self-actualization, seeking powers of godliness themselves, they become anti-god. Humanity must be reminded over and over again of their lowly state and their need to please the Source for all that they receive in life. Those who forget this must be sought out and destroyed so they do not infect others with notions of blasphemy and heresy.

"Many will survive the cleansing who do not have the capacity for understanding as you do. These blessed souls need merely to be taught and reminded by you of the priesthood. They will turn to you, to represent them before the Source. You are stewards of their well-being and as such must know what is best for them to keep them in the graces of the Source.

"There is no such thing as a natural disaster. There is only defined grace where all is well, and acts of god to bring the people back into alignment with the will of the Source. They must always turn to the Source, acknowledging his power, worshiping him as the source of everything. They must never forget that it is only by the will of the Source that they exist, and by his will, they can be destroyed.

"Now, are there any questions?"

Teuton fidgeted. His body was trying to give him feedback, but he was too much in his mind with the experience. He was triggered back into times of his religion experience. He asked, "What about morality?"

Shaweah answered, "Moralities are important keys of obedience. It is through morality that obedience is proven in personal conduct.

"For instance, the Source created humanity with the most powerful of drives for procreation. This is a most powerful tool for the privileged of the priesthood. Those who can successfully override their sexual drives must intensely turn to the Source to achieve such a feat. Those who demonstrate chastity and celibacy are chosen to advance into the priesthood and secret councils of the true religion.

"For those who do not successfully repress their sexuality, it is linked with the most powerful of emotions. It cannot be tolerated for people to enjoy their sexuality without it being linked to guilt and shame. People without guilt and shame who enjoy their sexuality for pleasure and connection to another person may erroneously believe the closest they can come to connecting with god is to connect with another human. They forget to worship and give credit to the Source. Those who practice sexuality without the repressions and inhibitions given by the Source aggrandize themselves, seeking for themselves attributes of godliness. They will seek to eliminate the necessary controls of the elite, who are privileged to the secrets and the priesthood.

"Loathsome, fearful, guilt-ridden, shameful emotions must be linked with sexuality. This way, sexuality will not become a substitute for worshiping in the true religion.

"Truth and accuracy are not the same. You need accuracy for mathematics, but truth is needed for religion. To speak the truth means to repeat the doctrines and dogmas, and to live the truth means to practice rituals and tenants of the true religion. A person is speaking the truth when they are repeating the truths they have been told by their chosen leaders. Failure to do so is to lie."

Teuton was becoming impatient with the channeling, but he was unsure how his impatience might affect Sequoia. He didn't want to trigger the hurt she had known as a teenager, and yet at the same time, he felt increasingly disturbed with what the beings who were channeling through Sequoia were saying. He decided to make an attempt to bring the session to an end.

"Shaweah, divine holy one, you have given us much information, and our meager human intellects need time to absorb your information before receiving more. May we make an appointment for another visit for your instruction?" Teuton asked.

"Yes. Until our next visit, be well," Shaweah concluded.

Teuton watched in anticipation to see what would happen with Sequoia next. She sat quietly for a few moments and then, with a start, shuddered and began blinking her eyes, as if she were returning to her body. Her eyes looked around the room, meeting the eyes of each other person and finally meeting Teuton's eyes. There was a deep look of concern in Teuton's eyes and a look of insecurity in Sequoia's.

She spoke first, saying, "Amigo, I think I'd better watch the replay of what just happened before we talk about it. Is that okay with you?"

Teuton replied, "*Si, mi amiga*. I think the rest of us have something to do. When you're ready, let us know, and we'll come together to discuss it."

To Sequoia's relief, Scera appeared at her side. "Let's watch the video of the channeling thing," she said.

Teuton went to join Redbird in the cockpit.

The entire crew had headphones on, so all could be included in the conversation.

Sequoia started off the discussion: "Has anyone ever experienced anything like this before?"

No one responded.

"Then let me explain it to you. We don't know if this kind of thing has always happened throughout history or not, but in recent times, beings who are not having lifetimes in bodies, like we are right now, speak through the bodies of people, recently called channels, who allow their bodies to be used for this. So I was getting the feeling that someone wanted to speak through me, and I decided to go along with it, with Teuton there to protect me.

"People assume anyone who speaks from the other side knows things that we don't know, especially about the future. One of the reasons they believe that is when these beings are channeled, they often say things about people that no one could have known. It is a pretty convincing way of getting people to listen. One of the really sad things is how many people are eager to believe in something and will totally buy into whatever is channeled, without deciding for themselves whether the being is actually speaking from higher wisdom.

"These beings usually make predictions. People are especially enchanted by hearing predictions. It seems to create a following very easily. Given a little time, most of these predictions fail to happen. The usual explanation for this is that these beings are living outside of time as we know it and therefore interpret time differently. Many of these predictions are long, long, overdue, and eventually the followers are lost, even though some of their wisdom might be helpful to people.

"Some very popular channeled entities have declared ongoing sensational information people have really bought into, which was utter nonsense. It shows how people are eager to believe that which is absurd and sensational over that which is reasonable. It is one of the mysteries of human beings, how we are eager to believe that which is sensational, and that which makes us afraid, without reality-testing the information. The bigger and more outrageous the lies are, the more people seem to believe in them, and act on them, as if they were true. You cannot convince them that it isn't true, when they are passionate about believing it."

Monique uttered, "Yes, you are telling us that just because someone doesn't have a body but wants to say something to us, it isn't any better than talking with anyone else, or reading any other opinion or viewpoint. Do we always have to decide for ourselves? That's really difficult, but all you have to do is enter something on a search engine, and anything anybody has put on the Internet is there for you to see. They can be lying, or they can be wrong, and people don't know."

Casey added, "That's the really difficult thing. How do you decide what is correct, and what is not correct? The Internet doesn't have a truth filter. I hear older people say that you used to be able to believe what was in print, and now anybody can write anything, and there isn't an editor or a publisher who decides whether it is worth publishing for people to consider. On the Internet, everybody gets to say whatever they think; and they can lie, or cheat, or steal, without people even knowing who's doing it."

Sequoia responded, "Yeah, it's really frustrating, isn't it? It's impossible to know whether the information that comes up is correct or not. We really have to check it out and, in the end, check it out with our own inner sense of knowingness."

Casey implored Sequoia, "So if teaching is reminding people of what they already know on a deeper level, and we have to check information out with our own inner sense of knowingness, why can't we just get that information from within ourselves?"

Sequoia thought a few moments before answering the question. "Are you always aware that you know, Casey?"

"No, I'm not. That's what I'm really confused about. How am I supposed to be the one who decides if something is right or not, when

I know that I don't know, yet people are saying that part of me *does* know? I really don't get this."

Even more challenged, Sequoia looked within for a deeper answer. She considered the mystery of her own knowingness, which came from a space of not knowing and not needing to know. Sequoia knew the most profound healings, the most profound changing of energy, really comes from the void, not from what she would consider herself. Sequoia let go of thinking she knew anything that would teach Casey and just began to speak:

"I've been working on understanding this all of my life. Sometimes, I get it so right, and sometimes, I think I'm right and I miss. I know the more I try to make something happen, the more difficult it is to make it happen. Letting it happen works better. My ego wants to know, and my ego wants to be right, my ego wants to be a great teacher, because my ego loves to be special, but when I come from my ego, I am most likely to miss the target.

"I am finding that if I remember its okay not to know, and honor the fact that sometimes I cannot know, and never will know, because some things are just unknowable, I see before me the great void, the great nothingness. For me, it's a place of blackness, a place from which creation comes, a place that contains all possibilities. From that space is every solution, every answer, but more importantly every question. When I question without the need for answers, I am amazed at what comes from the void.

"I'm not sure if I have even begun to speak to your question. I really don't think anyone can solve these mysteries for anyone else. You have to practice life to solve life's most basic mysteries. It would be nice if someone could just download everything we need into our minds, or we could learn facts that would always provide us with the correct answers whenever we need them. I think that's what we all want. The more we think we have that, the more closed we are to what we don't know. But more difficulty comes when we know that we don't know but think someone else does know. We hope that they know, we want something to believe so it is settled for us, and we give our power away to anyone who steps up to the podium and says they do know.

"The Internet is a great teacher. It has created a place that throws the responsibility for knowing what is valid back upon the seeker. It's so easy to see all of the different viewpoints, knowing they can't all be right. And we wonder sometimes if any of them are right.

"Maybe it's a constant state of asking, rather than a state of deciding what's right, that's important. Maybe what we really need is to always remind ourselves it is too soon to know. We get a sense of direction, and we go with it, and we try it out, knowing it is too soon to know, all the while we are practicing it, putting it to the test.

"I'm thinking that to be in the flow, it's more about checking within to find out what to go with, for the time being, rather than a decision that stops all exploration or all practice. If we remind ourselves it is too soon to know, we have to keep asking as we keep experiencing.

"Is that any use to you, Casey?"

Casey replied, "Yeah, I get that. It's like in mathematics; how basic math involves precise facts that have precise numbers and produce precise answers. Life isn't always that way. The more advanced math considers variables. As the variables change, the answers change, but the answers are never steady. The answers will always change in relationship to the variables."

"Wow!" Sequoia exclaimed. "That's like saying there aren't really answers, all there are is measurements along the way. So maybe what we're really doing is choosing the way, not the answer.

"I like that. It makes me feel good. There is so much pressure to decide upon an answer and stick with it. I like the idea of choosing a way, and going with that way, while at the same time being aware of the results, which are not final results, but simply measurements along the way. Then if the measurements are not acceptable to me, I can make adjustments, which can also include deciding to try another way.

"Have we arrived at something that works for you, Casey? It sure is working for me. I am understanding much clearer now."

Casey thought for a moment and then said, "Back to this channeling thing. I was looking at your body, Sequoia, and hearing different voices and personalities. Were you putting on an act?"

Sequoia smiled as she thought about her reply. "That was a loaded question. I have seen it happen where people claimed to be channeling as a clever way to manipulate people. They used channeling as an irrefutable source of information. The people they wanted to manipulate would be hearing the information as coming from a source that is unquestionably correct. That happens.

"I also think that a great deal of channeling is because the person who is the channel cannot understand or accept the difference between the life they are living and the wisdom within them on some other level. So they go into a trance, setting their outward personality aside, and a deeper, wiser level of themselves speaks, as if it were someone else. It uses a name and an identity that the outward personality can accept. The outward personality would have all kinds of difficulty if it had to accept that this deep level of wisdom and knowing is also part of who they are. So in these cases, there isn't really someone on the other side, or in another dimension, speaking through them at all. It's just another part of who the person that is channeling is.

"Now I'm taking a roundabout way of answering your question, because I was the one sitting there that you were looking at, while all of this was going on. You are probably wondering what I was doing."

"Yeah," Ersaline interrupted. "Like I was wondering where you were. How does a female body talk in a deep man's voice?"

"Since I know about these things I've just explained to you, I've been really suspicious of myself, as I watched the playback of what you saw. I have to be really clear and honest with myself. Is there something within me that wanted to pretend to be god almighty? Is there something within me that wanted to create a religion? Is there something within me that wanted to correct all religion? And how much of what went on is really something I wish I could do, and when I was in a trance I gave myself permission to go ahead and do it?"

"Like, that's so the point," Ersaline said. "You could be doing anything. Why would we believe you, like, at face value?"

Monique burst out with "I think god can talk for himself. He's supposed to have all those powers. He can use them instead of pretending through normal people."

"Yeah," Ersaline asserted, "what's with this god thing? Can't god talk to all of us and keep updating what he's got to say? God has to talk through his chosen people? If it is really there, why doesn't he just make it simple?"

Sequoia took the opportunity to get back on subject. "See, I have to keep the questions going so I don't deceive myself. If I deceive myself, I may also become pretty convincing to deceive you."

Casey asked Sequoia very pointedly, "Okay, what was going on?"

Sequoia sat deep in thought, unsure of how to answer Casey or the others. The weight of personal responsibility morphed from one form to another. She felt remorseful for bringing this experience before those she loved so much.

Teuton had made his way back from the pilot's seat and sat in on the conversation.

From his deep connection with Sequoia, he felt it was time to lift the burden from her—not to rescue her, but to support her as part of her life team. He checked in with his heart, feeling the intensity of his love for Sequoia. He wanted to be careful that whatever happened next would be an exploration, a discovery, that Sequoia would feel safe and protected all the while. He finally spoke up: "Let's all explore this situation together. Let's look at it from each of our own truths as best we can. I think we can arrive at a point of understanding and decide together how to interact with what has happened through Sequoia."

Sequoia felt vulnerable as she tilted her head sideways, gazing into Teuton's eyes with a look of deep love and appreciation. At this moment, he was certainly the captain of her life team.

Scera opened the discussion: "Am I supposed to feel guilty, ashamed, or wrong in some way, for living in my own power? I know what it's like to feel powerless; I think we all have. I would rather go to hell for being wrong about spirituality and religiousness, than to give up the power that I've been growing into all of my life."

Gabriel said, "I think it would be hell to be worshiping and appeasing some egocentric and narcissistic god that needed to be stroked and pleased all the time. I think I would feel more in my own power, refusing to give him what he wants. I really don't care whether he's pleased or not. If he's got that kind of power, he's only made noise about it. He hasn't been consistent about demonstrating it, if he ever did at all."

Redbird added, "I'll admit, I really want something to believe in. That offered me something to believe in, and it seemed to be supported by history too. Do we dare discount history and all the religions that have elements of what they said?"

Gabriel continued, "Religion has been the biggest reason for war throughout history. I don't think it was really the reason. The reason goes deep into every person. War is just the collective expression of all of us. Religion is just a pretense for war, the outward appearance that historians have recorded. If there was ever a religion that was valid, why would they be insecure and care about whether anyone else believed what they did? Why would a god want to destroy those who don't accept what they say? Wouldn't accuracy be validation enough … if religious accuracy really exists?"

Redbird replied, "In the Ten Commandments, it says that god is jealous and doesn't want any other gods before him. That's what we saw. That's consistent."

Gabriel retorted, "Is history a valid measuring device for the present? We can't even put it to the test, and we certainly cannot understand the meaning of something from a millennia ago, with language that keeps evolving and the meanings of words even sometimes reversing. We see that in our own lifetimes."

Teuton said, "Let's be careful we don't get into the unresolvable discussion of all time. We're concerned about what we heard. Let's measure the merits of the beings, and what they said, against our own sense of accuracy, in the here-and-now."

Sequoia took a turn to speak: "I have a hunch those entities could be the same ones who visited mankind in the past. Those they came through became known as prophets and wrote about it. We know the prophets were often not well received. I can see why the people resisted."

Saladin said thoughtfully, "Okay, let's assume what happened is something that has been repeating through history, and they are the same entities. Does that mean we have to take them as seriously as history suggests they've been taken through the millennia? What if, in a way, they are what they claim to be, only because they have been given energy by human beings by way of the adoration and worship and so on, that humans have done in their name? One of the things we've discovered is that because energy obeys human thought, when humans have a belief, and that belief has form, the energy of the belief will at least create the illusion that the form is real."

Redbird interrupted, "So if some beings who are not in body needed energy to conquer and rule out there in the universe, they would need to set up a belief system with humanity that would ensure a constant supply of energy, through the devotion of humankind. Right? And as long as they were getting that energy directed their way, they would have great power to focus on what they want to. This would make them appear to be the godhead they claim to be."

Scera spoke up, saying, "Everything they said was all about humanity giving their energy to what they claim to be, the source. They were all about squashing anyone who might explore having the same characteristics and abilities they have. They had some pretty strong methods for discouraging and punishing anyone who might seek to develop themselves and discover that these attributes of godliness were in everyone."

Jaing quickly jumped in with, "Just think what would happen if humanity caught on to this and quit giving this godhead their energy. The godhead would become an enemy to mankind and try to reconquer man for the energy they need to maintain their position."

Taj added, "What if it's always been about some beings who were very ambitious, about taking power and control out there in the galaxy, and came up with a plan to get energy directed to them for their desires?"

Ashwini declared, "This is beginning to sound like a science-fiction movie."

Viplow added excitedly, "Maybe that's all it ever was. Maybe these guys made up this whole thing so they could have the ultimate power. If someone can write science fiction now, who is to say science fiction wasn't being written before?"

Ashwini replied, "But don't we all know someone who has incorporated into their belief system the ideas that were first written for *Star Trek* and other futuristic science-fiction entertainment? Many contemporary spiritual ideas have become popularized through entertainment."

With the delight of discovery, Elekcia added, "That would be the ultimate con job. Just think how much has been stolen from humanity if this is, indeed, a ruse for power. This god is a fraud!"

Teuton decided to contain where this discussion was going. "I've never heard such discussion before. It could be absolutely right, or we may be creating another science fiction. What I want to know from this group is whether it is essential for us to go where we are going. Everyone take a moment to look within for an accuracy check."

Redbird was the first to speak up. "I think it's fundamental to what went on here today, to question the possibilities and the motivations behind this visit, because it actually demands we either make a choice to buy into it or to reject it."

Taj said, "If we reject it, and they are right, they are going to punish us in some way, probably eliminating us. If we live in fear that thought, their alleged power, then they get exactly what they want from us: a continuation of the supply of human energy."

Sudheer was feeling defiant and rebellious. "If we take the chance and reject them in favor of our own power," he said, "and nothing happens, we know we are not bound to their religion."

Scera added her vote: "My inner sense of correctness is very strong to keep going the direction I've been going in my life, as the most correct thing for me."

Sequoia said, "If I buy into their religion, I would be giving up all that I came into this life with, and all the progress of my life. I continually realize the goddess energy within me, and I know it produces results I, and other people, feel good about. I have a great deal of clarity about how my life has been going. As I review what was channeled through me, I get a dark, cloudy, confused feeling. I feel like my energy is being sucked away from me. Forsaking myself and jumping into their religion is not for me."

Casey added, "I know when to avoid a trap. I don't want their religion."

Sudheer spoke next: "Think about the offer they just made us. They just offered us power and prosperity, playing upon our greed and personal ambition, to get us to carry out their stuff. It is a little bit like being offered a winning lottery ticket. I see it for what it is, though. I choose to leave it alone."

Monique made her declaration: "Men and women are to be equal. My heart feels strong when I think of ignoring everything they had to say."

Teuton was the last to speak: "Okay, our inner guidance systems are all in harmony.

"One more important item of business: Sequoia took a risk to allow this experience so we could be challenged and come to a stronger sense of who we are as spiritual beings. Personally, I feel deep gratitude to Sequoia for placing herself out there at risk. I like the outcome of it all and think it has brought us closer together as a team. If you feel as I do, please join me in giving Sequoia three cheers."

Tears streamed down Sequoia's cheeks as she received the healing of hearing three cheers over the intercom; each member of the flight gave her a hug, expressing their gratitude for having the experience.

CHAPTER 9

———⌇⌇⌇⌇⌇⌇⌇———

There was something unusually quiet about Sequoia. Teuton felt her distance and thought it best to give her space.

"Hey, has anyone noticed how much time has gone by since the channeling?" Redbird asked.

"I think we all made the right decision," Gabriel added.

"Guess we don't have to worry about anything they said, either," Redbird came back with.

Scera suggested, "Just don't give them any more energy. If you don't think of them, if you stay focused in the moment, you won't be giving them any of your energy. Wouldn't you rather choose who and what you give energy to?"

Redbird thought about it and added, "Since the unmanifest is the source of all creation, from which energy flows, it must be the real source. It doesn't need anything to charge it with energy. It has everything to give."

Jaing contributed, "That could also be a reason few people have ever heard of, and even fewer understand, the concept of a space of nothingness, which, because it isn't limited by anything, contains the energy of all possibilities. Pretty weird concept, huh?"

Sudheer added, "As we give form and definition to things, we're also creating limitations. We think we are making something, and all the while we are making exclusions too."

Elekcia said, "You are stretching my mind here, Sudheer. Give me a break. If I want to tell someone about the void, or the unmanifest, or the abyss, I want to tell them something about it. I need to give them examples of what it's like so they can comprehend it. You're not giving me anything to comprehend with. What does it have to do with right now?"

Sudheer came back with, "Okay, whether you believe in it or not doesn't matter; if you're thinking about it, if you're talking about it, if you're pondering it at all, that's giving it energy. Whether you're for it or against it, you are really pouring energy into it."

Ashwini said, "Do you guys realize you're still giving energy to it? You still aren't letting go of the channeling experience. You want to process it and continue giving it energy? You may not be singing songs of praise and worship, you may not be praying to whoever that was, they are still winning energy from you."

"That takes me somewhere else. Is it okay to talk about it?" Viplow questioned.

"Can't say, without you first telling us about it," Jaing replied.

"Okay. The media has become a stronger influence on people's energies than anything else. By what they choose to present, it easily directs what people will give energy to. Only there is so much media, there's hardly any big focus of energy at all. It takes a disaster to bring a big focus.

"All right, I'm having a difficult time getting to what I was thinking about. Let me see if I can make it simple.

"First, either we've been part of the godliness that worked together to make creation, or it was the job of an omnipotent godhead."

Casey was in synch with Viplow and continued the thoughts: "Second, we're still broadcasting energy like we did when we were working together on creation, possibly more as we've continued on. If we are the creations, all creative energy is still dependent on the godhead."

Continuing in the telepathy Jessica continued, "Third, if there was an original sin, it was forgetting who we are and therefore chaotically wasting creative power. But if it all comes from a creator godhead, it isn't our fault! The only option we have is to appease this godhead and hope for favor."

In the flow of creating together, Elekcia concluded, "Fourth, it could be that our own misdirected creative energy is setting off unpredictable weather and natural disasters, without our realizing it. But the godhead could be manipulating the weather and movements of the planet surface. Possibly the godhead created our planet in a faulty state, so it continues uncorrected."

Scera said, "That's the simple version? Please don't get complicated on me, people."

Saladin said, with impatience in her voice, "Just drop the godhead thing. I think we can advance from the anthropomorphic relic. It's already been beaten to death; how much more do you need to beat it? You're thrashing about trying to fight with nothing, just a fraud."

Sudheer tried to summarize: "What I really want to get at is, if we all got a clue about who we are and what we are able to do working together, we'd have the power to change what people have been begging the godhead to do for millennia."

"Is anyone trying to force the students to be ready for them, the teacher?" Redbird asked. "I thought when the student is ready, the teacher will appear."

"Naw, Sudheer, I get what you're saying," Redbird replied. "When we get together with like-minded people, our godly creative powers still work. You just want us to go back to working together, like we did creating the universe."

"Hey," Jasmine said, "like, I think we've got trouble. Like, I know you can't see above, behind, and under from the cockpit, but the monitors are showing something like a big monster made of like clouds and lightning, overcoming us, about to swallow us."

Those who weren't piloting rushed to the sofa to see the monitors of the entire area around the plane. Gabriel and Saladin switched through different camera views.

"Is that for real?" Jaing asked.

"There's nothing visible from the cockpit," Scera said, puzzled. "The radar shows something holding position in front of us. Don't have a visual on it."

"Wait, a face is appearing … a human face! Do you see it, Redbird? Am I hallucinating?"

"No, I see it. What kind of UFO is it? It's there, but it doesn't seem to have material substance … like a hologram. The skies are getting dark. We're at cruising altitude. Clouds can't darken the sky like that up this high."

"All our screens are dark. No sign of light," Viplow said into his microphone.

"You have disobeyed me!" a commanding voice roared. "I'll show you my power! You will obey me!"

Teuton bristled. The warrior in him instantly responded to the challenge. He noticed a flow of adrenaline in his body. He felt ready to do battle. In the moment, he realized he was powerful. Something seemed like a big, blown-up display to instigate fear. He felt boldness. He felt protective. He felt his Oneness. He saw the being who spoke, an individual expression of Oneness, who was exploring the possibility of playing a role of taking other individual expressions energy to get more power and substance. He saw the biggest thief ever trying to take over Oneness itself. He saw a single individual expression, just like all others playing out a unique possibility of keeping others frightened in the dark while he stole their light.

"Who are you?" Teuton demanded.

"I am your god!"

"Oneness does not mean one god! You are a fraud!" Teuton said firmly.

"I will destroy you with my power!"

"I am prepared to fight you. I am standing against you. My power is increasing by your resistance to me. You must fight me!" Teuton challenged.

Teuton was standing in the cockpit side passageway, just out of the sofa's space. He was in a warrior stance, without weapons. Everyone watched intently. The drama brought them into the moment fully … no thoughts, just watching Teuton face the most feared being ever known to mankind.

"No one has ever gone against me and survived."

"You lie," Teuton replied. "No one has ever stood against you? Whoever you fight will get your energy, be strengthened. You're on the offense. I get your energy. I am becoming more powerful. You are spending your power and giving me more power. Soon, I will be more powerful than you!"

In a moment of silence, Teuton realized the god knew speaking lies weakened himself, and Teuton speaking truth increased strength.

"Speak to me! If you are the source, what fear do you have of not having enough energy to remain more powerful than me?"

The black skies started flashing wildly. The plane began to pitch with turbulence. Teuton braced himself. The others sat down and buckled in. There were tormenting screeches and howls with thunder.

"You see my power?" the god roared.

"A human can do that," Teuton retorted. "How much power did it take you to put on that display? Are you a child having a temper tantrum? You didn't hurt me, you gave me more power."

Again the skies flashed; it sounded like every horror movie combined on steroids. The plane jumped and shook.

"I am telling everyone you're just a fraud, no more than anyone else, and they will see you've made them small through your belief systems. They'll have their power because they quit giving away their power to you. You will be average, normal, what you always were!"

"I am the Source! I am inexhaustible."

"You weaken yourself with every lie you tell! I am strengthened with truth! I will enable everyone to find truth, and they will be more powerful than you!"

"I will destroy you!" The whole plane shook.

Everyone else was quiet. They were holding space for Teuton. Sequoia had gone off alone.

"Give me your best shot," Teuton challenged. "If you speak truth, why have you not already done so? You can't have someone kill me for you. You can't have someone else do what you can't do. Your powers are lies! Embodied individual expressions of Oneness have more power than you. Your ruse is exposed! You seek the power of the embodied because you don't have that kind of power."

"You will die!"

"I get that, but what are you waiting for? I am still standing here!"

"I am your god! I created you! I created Oneness."

The skies were showing some light, becoming gray. Scera saw a horrible image of a grim reaper flying at the plane from in front, presumably disappearing into the plane's interior. It challenged her holding presence. Words started to form and then she returned to noticing. The grim reaper wasn't in the moment.

"Are you finished with Hollywood stunts?" Teuton demanded. "I am here for a battle, and all I get is lies, nothing real, nothing with which I can do battle! I can't fight effects! Energetic holograms cannot do anything to me! Where is your essence?"

"I am."

"Let's give a description to what you are! Then let's drop all the concepts of you that have no essence."

"I am everything."

"Then you are Oneness, just like me and just like every part of godliness. You are no more than anyone, but you don't have the power of someone incarnate."

The skies were clearing up. The illusions were losing appearance. Teuton stood in his power, unchallenged.

"Was fear your essential tool?" Teuton asked. "Lies and appearances to create fear to get energy? I stand before you in my truth, ready for your challenge, and nothing is showing up to meet me. Is it you who are afraid now?"

Teuton grew in courage and determination.

"You were always a fraud! You needed so much energy because you didn't realize your own connection with Oneness! You're lost in separation! With each lie, you become weaker ... your effects weaken. Your effects are lies too!"

Weakened but continuing to act the part, the god said, "You will never defeat me! I fill a void in mankind, a desire they seek outside themselves to find. I have armies of priests and politicians who need what they think I am, what they want me to be! They will never let you finish me."

Sounding as if he were finishing an enemy, Teuton spoke in his power, saying, "Then they created you! You aren't even an individual expression of Oneness. You're no more than a hologram of lies with a form of power you have been given by those who actually have the power. You are the lie they create that gives them exactly the lies they've created you with."

Not giving up, the god seemed sure of his existence and said, "No one will believe you. They don't know what truth is. You are just another fool who thinks someone else knows what truth is. They will kill you for bothering their consolations. They will kill you for me. They want me. They created me. I am their expression, everything they want. They won't tolerate you destroying that in them.

"You I cannot defeat. You I cannot do battle with. You don't desire me. I am not real for you. But to my loyal creators, I am real, and they will defeat you for me!"

Teuton noticed the story had no more in it. He walked to the front of the plane, went into the rear of the cockpit, and sat on the jump seat. The view outside the cockpit was normal, the instruments were normal. No one was speaking.

He thought of Sequoia. He wondered how it was he who stood up to the illusion of god. Sequoia was the usual guru. He began to realize their psychic connection was there, but he hadn't been in telepathy with her. He wondered what that meant as he arose from the jump seat and walked toward the staircase.

He went down the stairs to the sofa and was surprised to see everyone sitting there except Sequoia. He walked back to the berths. She wasn't there. He stopped to search the moment for a sense of her. He couldn't feel her.

He went forward to the four deprogramming stations. Sequoia lay there in a heap, as though she'd lost all energy and collapsed onto the floor. He rushed to her.

He moved her head, arms, and legs to help her circulation. He checked for pulse and breathing.

Finally, she moved and mumbled his name. She opened her eyes and said, "I'm so sorry, amigo. I should never have come against you."

"What do you mean? What happened to you?" Teuton asked.

"Amigo, I believed I was beyond the rest of you. My entitled privileged lifetimes were filled with being special and privileged with god. We always promoted the god, believing it kept us special with god. We have lived as gods, getting energy and resources from others. We believed god wanted it that way, and it was our duty.

"Are you okay?" Teuton asked with deep concern. He thought she'd served others. His memory of being privileged made sense with what she was saying, though.

"Help me onto one of the deconditioning machines you perfected," she said.

Teuton scooped her into his arms. She laced her fingers together behind his neck as he lifted her to the table.

"I'm the exception," she said weakly. "I'm the only one who hasn't had the energy bundles dissipated. I wasn't deprogrammed from the media subliminals. No one ever questioned my need."

"Was the god I stood against your projection?"

"Yes," she responded. "You defeated that energy in me. I've seen my shadow, and my shadow was no match for your integrity."

"Amiga, I am sorry. I would never harm you."

"I know that. The false, the shadow in me chose to try to keep you small and frightened. On the island, I was in the role of power; when I kidnapped you, there was unequal power. We've always been unequal in power. You couldn't make love to me, because I feigned the power of being celibate. For thousands of years, my ancestors have been rulers, wealthy and privileged, and looked up to as powerful. The energy of it is in me, and I didn't want it disturbed. I welcomed you as my partner, a serf to a princess, but there was always unequal power. I called in the ultimate power against you. I watched what was in me as I played out everything I wasn't willing to have disturbed to maintain my position with all of you."

"I can see that," Teuton said thoughtfully. "I'm not more powerful than you. I defeated illusions. I defeated nothing. I have always loved you, and I welcome you more fully as my partner."

"I'm afraid to give up what makes me separate. I'm afraid of what I'm going to lose."

"I celebrate what you're gaining," he said softly.

"Amigo, quit trying to take care of me. I need to confess this and let it be seen in its nakedness. I know you love me. Hook me up to this machine and operate it. I want to step into the real with you. I want to give up whatever I have to so I can know my essence in Oneness, as you do. If you quit taking care of me, you'll see I observe you being more authentically real and in truth than me. You accepted a lifetime of hardship, relinquishing and doing whatever it would take to move beyond your barriers. I want to follow you, my best friend."

Teuton understood. Sequoia closed her eyes as he silently went to work, attaching meridian points to the machine and surrounding her head in the helmet. He carefully closed the casing around her, checked for air circulation, and moved to the control panel.

After Sequoia's session, Teuton led her to her sleeping berth and then respectfully left her to rest. When he returned to the sofa, the others had gone to other places in the plane, and he was alone.

Teuton felt at a loss. He could busy himself, researching something or learning a new subject. If he wanted, he could plan a workshop. Withdrawing into his own busy-ness was not appealing. He found no motivation within himself to be busy with any of his usual occupations, which he usually did to distract himself from his need for connection and affection. He thought of being with one of his lovers but didn't feel the appeal.

He sank into the sofa and closed his eyes.

Several dreams appeared and disappeared, without a recognizable theme. He began to realize he was in a dream of a surreal place, a place of frustration. He was looking for Sequoia. He would catch a glimpse of her, but when he tried to go to her, there was no way to get there. Scene after scene played in his dream. He was someplace, and he could see where Sequoia was, but there was nothing between them he could use to get to her. Sequoia appeared to be oblivious to him. He couldn't let her know he wanted to be together with her. He couldn't get her attention or communicate with her in any way, so she might come his way. He felt trapped in an abyss. He began to feel desperate, to feel the pain of missing her, as if one of them had died, but he didn't know who.

He didn't know if it was he who was dead, watching her go on with life, but he suspected it might be so.

Next, a woman appeared beside him in a beautiful garden. She was exquisitely beautiful. Her voice was soft and soothing. She told him he had done well in life but failed the most essential of life's opportunities. She told him what a shame it was he failed to be total in love.

Teuton objected and spoke of his unconditional love, his loyalty, and his commitment to the betterment of mankind. He told her he often resonated with the love of godliness, feeling connected with everything in a warm feeling he knew as love. How could she say he failed at love?

Again, he saw Sequoia off in the distance. He thought this woman was an angel, helping him to review his life, thinking he was dead, but still being able to see Sequoia carrying on. The Sequoia he saw was somber, occupying herself with her work. He was no longer able to work with her.

He turned to his beautiful guide. He asked if he might continue to work with Sequoia as her guide, to inspire her, to help her through her life. Surely, he would now be able to help her with information from the other side. She could become one of the most brilliant scientists in the whole world, with his help.

The guide looked at him with sad eyes as she shook her head and said "no." Then Teuton found himself in a place filled with anguished people who lived lives without knowing love. He heard a voice say, "This is your place."

Teuton objected again. After all, he had known love. He had aligned himself with love, lovingly dropping judgment of others, and even in his practice of meditation, he had found himself in a receptive place of no-mind, where he felt filled in his heart.

A hand appeared, a very large hand, with its finger pointing to the middle of the crowd. Nothing was said. Teuton felt helpless, like a prisoner arrested and taken away from everything in his life, condemned, and thrown into jail, unable to settle any of his personal affairs, deal with any of his belongings, say good-byes, or visit his favorite places for the last time; just torn away … forced to continue living, without having his life.

Teuton awakened, feeling damp with sweat. He looked about himself and felt deeply grateful that in an instant, he was back in the life he knew. He felt the tremor building from within, as tears welled up in his eyes and began to stream down his cheeks.

He was grateful to find himself alone in the room.

He surrendered into the crying.

CHAPTER 10

———∿∾◦◦⪦⪧◦◦∿∾———

"What was that?" Scera exclaimed.

"What?" Redbird asked.

"Something flew past us," she replied.

Casey added, "Hey you guys, we're being followed. Just underneath and a little behind us is an airplane. Looks like a fighter plane. And look, behind us, there are some more."

Scera came back with, "We can't see anything from up here. What do you see on the screen?"

"I haven't been getting anything on the radio."

"See if you do any better when you turn the radio on," Redbird retorted as he reached forward to turn on the radios.

Scera asked, "Which frequency? It's going to take some time to figure out which frequency. Do they look like they might fire on us?"

"How would we know?" Redbird replied.

Teuton spoke up, saying, "That's a good sign; fighter planes don't carry much fuel, so unless they've been fueling off of a tanker, they came up from the ground not too long ago."

Redbird explained, "It won't be a very good sign if they shoot us down. Can you figure out whose planes they are?"

Viplow observed out loud, "Can't really see anything painted on their sides or tail, since we're mostly looking right into their noses. I can see the top of the wings of the one that's underneath us, but nobody paints insignia on the top of the wings."

Sequoia said, "If the radios aren't working, they are probably identifying all aircraft headed their way right now."

"Okay everyone, listen up," Gabriel commanded, "let's all get out of thoughts into moment awareness. Feel into your hearts. Let your heart expand its energy. If you're thinking, come back. Information and communication with all of us, including the pilots of those planes, is in the moment, not in words."

"One of them is coming over the top of us," Taj reported. "It's passing us."

"Okay, it's coming into view now," Redbird reported. "It's not American, not American made either. Must be European or Asian. There are Brazilian passenger planes, but do they make fighter planes? Think it's trying to force us down."

"Cut power and begin descent," Gabriel barked.

"It's not letting up. I think you're right, they want us to descend," Scera reported. "If they intend to take us all the way to the ground, I hope they don't think we can descend as fast as a fighter plane."

"Just keep in their formation, don't show any signs of noncooperation," Gabriel ordered.

Teuton instructed those who were not on the flight crew, "Look around you; we need to secure anything that's loose. Then come to the round sofa or classroom and buckle in. We need to be watching the screens to let the pilots know of anything that they can't see."

Sequoia said, "Okay guys, remember, we are supposed to survive. If we were meant to die, if this plane was not meant to fulfill its mission, we wouldn't be where we are right now. Expect that divine wisdom is taking us unexpectedly, to the important next step of our mission. Things have a way of working out the way that serves the highest good."

Everyone's eyes were glued to the screens, and Scera was carefully focused on watching the underside of the jet fighter, just slightly ahead of the nose of the plane. At high speeds, the slightest shift in direction or speed can result in a collision when planes are this close. Air Transport Pilots don't get any training in formation flying. At least with formation flying, there is radio contact. Scera could only anticipate and mimic the flight path of the plane outside her window. Redbird watched the instruments, knowing Scera couldn't break her focus for even a moment. A long turn indicated adjustment toward wherever they were being taken. With cloud cover over the entire area, it could only be guessed what the terrain was like below.

The pilots began to wonder if the other planes would be visible as they descended through the clouds. Never before was there another airplane near enough to know what visibility there might be when flying in clouds. As they were about to descend into the clouds, everyone was focused on visual contact with the fighter escorts. One mistake by anybody in those clouds could result in a rain of debris falling out of the clouds to earth.

Time lost all relevance. With a sky so vast and so much room for everybody to fly in, it just didn't make sense to crowd airplanes together. But how do you hold formation in clouds, where there might be turbulence in the first place, to say nothing of seeing where the other planes are? Scera's focus was in the moment, and knowing directing her motions without thinking about it.

Now the test of how well proficiencies practiced on Sequoia's island paid off in a life-threatening, real situation.

It seemed like the clouds were never going to end. No one lost their focus. If only a break in the clouds would show the position of the fighter planes, if only flying through the ceiling would bring relief from the imminent danger. With no information about weather, and no experience with tropical flying, there could be no expectation, too little information, only intuition could guide the pilot into whatever distance might be left to the ground, when visibility was regained.

No one spoke.

Descending below the clouds, the first thing visible through the cockpit windshield was the fighter plane in front of them. The plane's landing gear was out.

"Lower the landing gear," Scera ordered.

"Extend flaps," she ordered again.

"Everyone prepare for landing," she commanded.

"We should be approaching Manaus Air Base in Brazil," Gabriel said. "What do you see?"

Scera replied, "I don't see an airport yet. The fighter appeared to be prepared for landing, so we are prepared for landing." With that Scera added power to the engines to maintain speed behind the fighter. The fighter retracted its landing gear and quickly accelerated away. No longer intent on every motion of the fighter, Scera's focus extended forward to see an airfield ahead. There was a great sigh of relief. She skillfully entered the glide slope using the VASI lights at the beginning of the runway to get the descent onto the runway right.

Soon over the runway, she guided the plane into a skillful touchdown. Then she let the plane slowly taxi to the last exit off the runway before turning and rolling across the hold short line. Here, she let the engines idle.

"What did you all see as we came in?" Scera asked over the intercom.

Teuton reported, "I don't think I saw any other planes. Didn't look like there was an air terminal either. Saw plenty of parking and some really big hangers. There is a tower there but it's not very big."

"There's a vehicle moving our way," Gabriel reported.

An open Jeep drove down the taxiway. Only the driver was in it. It came to the end of the taxiway and made a U-turn, and the driver reached his hand high and signaled them to follow. So Scera gently applied power to follow the jeep. When the jeep came to a rest near the building with a tower rising above it, she powered off the engines.

From a hangar, a platoon of men with automatic weapons and missile launchers ran to surround them. They aimed their weapons at the plane.

Through the 360 degree panorama screens, Elekcia discovered that a metal ladder on wheels was being pulled by a tug out of the open door of the hangar. They watched as the driver brought it around to the starboard door of the aircraft, always used as the service door rather than moving passengers on and off the aircraft.

Knowing that, Teuton went to the front starboard door and opened it to receive the ladder and greet whoever was coming to meet them. The man who was driving the Jeep was now walking across the tarmac. He was wearing a military uniform. With his translating cell phone in hand, Teuton began descending the stairs to meet the man on the ground. One of the younger men could have easily been the representative to meet the hosts, but everyone knew Teuton's age would work in their favor.

As the man approached, Teuton noticed his brown eyes and reached out his hand in greeting. He had already recorded a greeting into the phone, so he pushed the button for the phone to play the greeting in Portuguese. The man replied in an unfamiliar language. Teuton pushed the button to hear the English translation of what the man said:

"Hello sir. Thank you for cooperating with our Mirage Fighters. We need to know what your business is flying into our airspace. Please come with me into our office."

With that, the man turned and started walking toward the building under the tower. Teuton was thinking it was strange that there were no other airplanes to be seen on the field. However, he quickly realized it may be because the Brazilians were in a state of emergency. He looked up into the tower, but he could not see through the smoky glass whether anyone was there. Soon they arrived at the door, which the man politely opened; a man in an officer's uniform was coming from the doorway of a room across the big foyer. As they reached out hands to greet, the officer introduced himself, speaking in accented English:

"Hello, I am Colonel Izique."

"I am Teuton."

"Are you the captain of this plane?" the colonel asked.

"No, the pilot is still in the plane. I am representative of the airline who owns this aircraft. This experimental plane is on a scientific expedition; I will be pleased to give you an inspection of the equipment on board. Perhaps also you will be so kind as to give us information of where we may continue our flight to one of your research facilities. We have information to share."

"Yes, Mr. Teuton. Thank you for your invitation. As you can see, there has been a state of emergency. All our aircraft are scrambled. There are unscheduled planes entering our airspace from the north and west, so all of our aircraft are intercepting and identifying the planes. Yours was of concern to our pilots, so they brought you here to this airfield. We don't know if there will be bombers or missiles coming to us, so we need to take every precaution we can. I hope you understand, sir."

"Thank you, sir. We thought that might be the purpose of your planes directing us here. In fact, we were fleeing North America because while we were in flight, it appeared as though atomic bombs were being detonated. Because of the effect on our radios, we couldn't get any news or information. We decided to flee south in hopes that whatever was going on was only going on in the Northern Hemisphere. As you know, most of the countries with atomic warheads are in the Northern Hemisphere. The threat of nuclear war has always been between northern countries. We understand your grave concern."

"It is a relief to talk with you, Mr. Teuton. Thank you for your cooperation. As you can see, I do not have personnel here on the field to do a thorough inspection of your plane. But I will be pleased to accompany you for a quick walkthrough, and I will ask you to open your baggage compartments please."

"Very well," Teuton said, "please come with me. Do you have any news about what has happened?"

Teuton led Colonel Izique toward the plane.

"I do not know if it is a blessing or a curse to get news. You know as well as I do that whenever there is a state of emergency, communication and travel in and out of an area is crippled until they are re-established. There was a sudden blackout of news and communications from the north. Our seismic equipment has recorded earth movement in many places of the United States, Europe, the Middle East, and across Asia. Here our communications are still working, but we cannot learn what is happening to the north."

"You have already told me a lot more than we knew, Colonel, and what I can tell you is the disturbances you have been reading were nuclear warheads going off," Teuton said. "There wasn't any publicized indication this was going to happen. And you have confirmed my fears that it didn't just happen in the areas we observed."

With that, Teuton courteously motioned for the colonel to ascend the ladder into the plane. Everyone was gathered just inside the plane, and they began introducing themselves to the colonel. Gabriel first took him to the left to show him his workstation. Then he took him into the galley and the bathrooms.

Next, Ashwini led the colonel down the staircase to the circular sofa, where Viplow explained the screens, which were showing a 360 degree panorama around the plane. He was then led into the sleeping quarters and through the door at the rear, where Gabriel explained the equipment. When they returned, Gabriel invited Colonel Izique to join with everyone in the classroom.

Teuton led the discussion: "Colonel Izique, as you can see, this plane contains information for scientific purposes. It has become known to us that in Brazil, research has been done on how to stop the radiation from nuclear blasts. We also have some technology for this purpose. We want to join with your people, share our information, and with great hope prevent all the radiation that has been unleashed in the Northern Hemisphere, from destroying all life on earth."

Colonel Izique tilted his hat and stroked his chin as he thought about what had been said. Then he looked up at the people sitting around him, looking into the face of each one of them. Then he spoke:

"I am a military man. Such a secret has also been kept from the military. However, in Brazil we experience life differently than much of the world. We have some exceptional healers, and yes, the people have been concerned about how innocent people will die from the actions of the imperialists in the north and terrorists. Please excuse me, but you people come from a military superpower, the country that makes the rest of us fear. It is mostly because of your country that we have made plans to defend ourselves. Of course, you are our allies. However, you never know when the bully who is your friend may decide to push you around. You always live in fear of your bully friends. I am sorry if this offends you."

"Colonel Izique, sir, the airline that owns this plane, which we represent, is very international. Many members of C-Know are Brazilian, and others are from other countries in South America. A plane exactly like this one has been flying regularly to and from Brasilia. Not only that, but we have five more planes. We have no political or military affiliations whatsoever. Our intention is to preserve mankind in case of a worldwide catastrophe.

"We just happened to be going to Madagascar over the North Pole before the bombs started exploding. I am sure you know that what the

173

atomic bombs have not destroyed with explosions, they will destroy with radiation.

"If you will please, sir, work with me, I have contact information for Brazilian members of C-Know," Teuton said. "C-Know and its work have been kept secret until a time like this when it was to be revealed. Colonel, you are the first person that we know of that this secret has been revealed to. Now we will reveal it to everyone, because the conditions under which it was to be revealed have happened."

"Then come with me to my office," the colonel replied, "and we will make contact with these people. Perhaps a Brazilian member of your C-Know can take you to meet the scientists with this secret radiation technology you say we have. This is as much help as I can give you."

Upon hearing this, everyone in the room began thanking Colonel Izique, reaching their hands to shake his. After a few moments, he led Teuton into his office.

"Okay, here is our flight plan, instructions, and contacts," Teuton said. "When we arrive in Rio, we will be met by someone who will speak with us about dealing with radiation and radioactive fallout." He handed the papers to Gabriel. "Colonel Izique was helpful, but I'm sure we're going to be scrutinized carefully when we get to Rio. After all, what would be the reason for them to just start cooperating with someone who says they know about one of their most top secret projects?"

The pilots taxied the plane to the beginning of the runway and then they were cleared for take-off. They had filed a flight plan to Rio, to be identified along the way by the Brazilian air traffic control system. There was static in the radios, but most likely the curvature of the earth was protecting the signals in the Southern Hemisphere.

It had been a long, stressful day and a half since this flight began. Except for the flight crew and Teuton, everyone went into the sleeping quarters to catch some rest before arriving in Rio.

CHAPTER 11

—————ww°º⊙⊙⊙⊙º⊙ww—————

Teuton first went into the shower, since everyone else had cleaned up while he and Col. Izique were busy making arrangements.

As the water droplets showered him in soothing warmth, he felt the water gently making its way over his fatigued body. He relaxed his head back, closing his eyes, feeling the water splashing on his crown chakra, dribbling down his forehead, making channels around his eyebrows, gently caressing his eyelids as his cheeks came alive to the warm flow of water. He opened his mouth to allow the welcomed water to fully course over his lips. His beard bristled, something he would soon soften with shampoo.

As he dried himself, he thought of Sequoia. He felt the familiar warmth in his heart as he thought of her. He envisioned her, seeing her in some of his favorite moods and expressions, seeing her in his mind's eye in the many ways he loved her. He winced a bit as he felt something within him pain, as his eyes welled up in tears. He remembered how he felt in the group hug.

As secure as Teuton knew his friendship with Sequoia to be, he feared it was loaded with an explosive device, an electronic relationship sensor that would destroy him and all he loved about Sequoia if he ever even had an intention of exploring a romantic relationship with her. So he treasured and guarded, always protecting, his love for Sequoia by honoring her celibacy.

After Sequoia lay in her sleeping quarters for a few minutes, she experienced a familiar yearning in her heart. Her thoughts went to

Teuton, the man she'd spent years with. She could feel a yearning begin to flutter in her heart. She had felt this yearning before; it betrayed her belief she was beyond sexual intimacy. Today, her desire for Teuton came from deep within her. In their friendship, they'd known the experience of connection and Oneness, and in the group hug, she found herself yearning for something deeper and more connected with him.

She realized she wasn't going to sleep easily. So much had happened to transform her. She had new feelings to ponder about her best friend, her amigo.

Her thoughts moved in a slow liquid flow. The thoughts stopped at a memory of earlier in the day, when she wanted to experience deeper Oneness with another human being, and she wanted to experience the part of Oneness she'd been denying herself: Oneness of body-soul connection. She felt the poignant and profound stirring in her heart and body to be closely connected with this man she'd been best friends with all these years.

Teuton paused in the galley to pour himself a glass of juice. Thoughts of the day, memories of the events, were echoing in his mind. He descended the stairway without thinking to look around him, turning toward the sleeping quarters. He noticed he was moving without forethought. He knew this well. He wasn't efforting it. He was just going with the moment, noticing what was happening. He witnessed himself moving smoothly and gracefully to where Sequoia was laying quietly on her bed with her eyes closed. He sat on the bed beside her.

As he sat there watching, his heart began to race, his palms were getting sweaty, and he could feel himself tremble. The small journey that lie before him seemed like the most difficult challenge he had ever faced.

Had he been able to allow it to be, there was a powerful heart response from the time they met, even when he wasn't remembering their significance together.

Year after year went by with him perfectly honoring her celibacy. Now Teuton was facing the most vulnerable moment of his life. He had to gamble, to win. He could now see what he thought was winning was actually a stalemate. He felt his hands quiver. His breath was short. His cheeks felt hot.

But she lay there sleeping. Until she awoke, he would have time to regain his composure, if ever he had any. And if the vulnerability proved to be too much, he could slip back out of the room as easily as he entered (or so he reasoned).

Something about the strand of Sequoia's hair falling across her face took Teuton's attention. He noticed her skin, just a little freckled on her cheeks. He noticed a curvature of her nose, following around her nostrils; suddenly, he felt he wanted to paint the picture of her beauty. Her eyelashes were long and curved upward. He'd never noticed this before. He wondered how eyelashes could be so attractive. He followed the curve of her nose to her eyebrows and forehead. He gasped just a little and felt his heart skip a beat, as something about the curves of her face excited him. He followed her hairline to her ear. Never before had he actually looked at her ear and seen the delicate beauty of it. He wondered at his blindness, as his eyes followed the curve of her jaw: down, around, and up to her lips. He felt like he could melt onto the floor. He suddenly realized he wanted to kiss those lips more than anything else in the world, right now. He studied her face as if he had never seen it before, and might never see it again. He studied her face as if no photograph could ever preserve for him the beauty of this moment, he must, he decided, capture in his mind.

Sequoia's hands were almost in a Namaste position. He noticed the delicacy of her little fingers. He felt a quiver run down his feet. He had never realized how beautifully formed her fingers were, how nicely rounded. And her natural fingernails were just long enough to be attractive, but not too long. Hers were his ideal of beautiful hands. He noticed the skin of her hands. He had touched those hands before; he had held those hands before, but not romantically. He felt butterflies in his stomach. He wanted those fingers interlaced with his. He wanted to kiss her hands. He began to fear what would happen if he let go of all the passion he felt, all at once.

Teuton had never felt taken by passion like this. Now, if he tried to stand up, he didn't even know if his legs would have the strength to hold him; he imagined he would stumble and fall and wake her if he tried to leave. He was trapped. Any moment that she awoke, he would be at her mercy.

As she lay dreaming, Sequoia saw a man standing across the campus, at least a hundred yards away. She felt her heart leap within her, as she found her feet beginning to carry her his way. He was beginning to run toward her, opening his arms. She danced as she ran and felt the joy of love overflowing. She had never felt so much excitement, yet she wondered who he was. She was in college again, she was young. That was a different time. That was a different life. But she was in it.

As she got close enough to see into his eyes, she knew him. She loved him. But it was strange that she didn't know him. Closer they came, both with outstretched arms. Her anticipation grew for the moment they would surely meet, spinning around and around in the joy of embrace, her feet floating in the air.

And just as the moment was about to happen, she awoke with a start. The eyes before her were eyes she knew. The eyes before her were eyes she loved. The face was older, more seasoned, and the face of her dreams, both waking and sleeping. She hardly noticed her hand reaching up, but she did notice the hand reaching toward her, and she didn't notice his trembling at all.

Sequoia's eyes softened as they filled with tears for a few moments more; they gazed into each other's eyes until she lifted a finger to wipe a tear that began to fall down her cheek. Then they both leaned in, their foreheads meeting, as they fumbled first to find each other's hands, only to release their hands and cup each other's faces with their thumbs across the cheeks to caress the wetness of streaming tears. Both began to quiver with the deep emotion finally freed to dance in the sunshine. Teuton let his hands drop to reach around Sequoia's body, caressing her back and gently pulling her toward him.

Quite naturally, as their bodies came closer, their heads began to tilt so first their noses met then slid beside each other as both became aware of the heat of the other's breath upon sensitive lips, just before the very first touch of lover's lips, slowly pressed together in the moment that would only unfold once: the first kiss.

Slowly and gently, lips parted as they pulled back to look into each other's eyes and see the new person who would be there, the new person born in that moment, honest and naked and vulnerable, having just opened their new life together. Then slowly, simultaneously, they both smiled in delight and started giggling.

There was no more thinking. Years of suppressed love was no longer contained. They clumsily searched for the second kiss, driven by passion shared, the passion of two people coming toward each other and having no place to go but to burst upward. And burst upward they did, into the most uplifting expression of their whole lives. Lips and tongues unleashed were exploring, giving and receiving tenderness and passion, sensuality and comfort, in deep gratitude to finally be finding the joy of bursting into intimacy with life's most beloved.

They were truly ageless as their passion flowed into each other; they eagerly searched each other's body with their hands, finding how awkward it was from skewed sitting positions. Teuton slid his hands down to Sequoia's waist as he made his way under her blouse to her skin. At her back, his hand slid up her spine to her shoulders, passing over her bra, as his front hand caressed her belly and lower ribs, squeezing and caressing.

Sequoia quivered but there was no parting of lips, not now, and not for a long time. Both had a sense of not letting go of the precious new status with each other they had so long wished for. Sequoia found Teuton's top button and hastily tugged at it to get it free. Teuton's hand slid down, as he fumbled the back of her bra, searching for its clasps. Then she reached to her bra with both hands to unhook the clasp between her breasts and raised her hands upward. He followed by pushing her blouse up over her shoulders, past her upper arms, and over her hands to freedom; he reached back down for her bra, also pulling it up, freeing Sequoia's arms to return to unbuttoning his shirt. Soon she was pushing his shirt off of his arms, lips still embracing the second kiss, as she felt pleasure coursing through her body.

They wiggled and rolled to find a place for playing together on the bed, preserving the sanctity of that second kiss they wanted to last forever. As their bare chests pressed against each other, pleasure ran through the totality of their being. They fondled each other and focused on deeply and passionately kissing for a minute. Then almost at the same moment, in the same thought, both slid a hand down the bare skin still covered by clothing. With movement restricted, they wiggled again to give just enough space for each other's hands to unlatch belts and pants to give room to reach within to pleasure one another.

Caressing and kissing, their passion built until Sequoia began pushing his pants off. Where she couldn't push with her hands she hooked with her toes until she had his legs completely unshackled.

Now it was her turn, as he began pushing the top of her pants around her hips as she assisted him, not wanting any delay in the pleasure of wrapping her bare legs around his. Still in a struggle, like a tug-of-war, feet and legs were thrashing until finally her pants were pushed free. Still their lips were clasped in their second kiss.

She pulled her knee up over the outside of his leg as they pushed their bodies together, taking her breath away with the pleasure. Meanwhile, Teuton's hands traced their way up her back to her shoulders, as he fanned his fingers into her hair, caressing her head. Their lips were partially unsealed as her breathing was getting heavier, yet they refused to let their lips part.

Sequoia arched her back as she pulled her hips upward with increasing passion. Their bodies were becoming slippery with sweat. The kiss was finding a new stage of intensity. Teuton's hands caressed her, giving her deep pleasure. She burst out in the moans and squeals of orgasm, nearly threatening the end of the second kiss, but that kiss was just not to be let go of.

Sequoia was moving her hips in a circular motion as Teuton pumped his lingam in thrusting motion as it slipped around the delight of her wetness. They were in no hurry to end this delightful pleasure. Sequoia once again burst into orgasm, pushing her mouth against his as she muffled her screaming expression of pleasure exploding within. He held her tight as her body twisted and jerked involuntarily in uncontrolled ecstasy. Then they lay together as she regained enough composure to begin moving again, continuing their dance of pleasure. Again she burst out while she writhed in coursing pleasure.

After a brief rest, the intensity increased as they moved faster, more passionately, wildly, and then they suddenly joined. Sequoia burst into another long orgasm, assisted by Teuton's motion. At last they were totally together, all the way, having each other in the greatest delight, the greatest pleasure, the most amazing ecstasy either one of them could have ever imagined. They let their passion carry them into the infinite.

They were taking the most amazing journey of their life into each other, and with each other, and all about each other, yet expanding into the infinite of the whole universe. Their hearts were so radiant it seemed like they were glued together by an electromagnetic force more powerful than all the strength both of their bodies might be able to muster. They were still preserving that second kiss, sometimes really focusing on the kiss, sometimes so focused elsewhere, preserving the kiss was all they managed to do.

Satisfied for the moment, they became aware of a tremendous presence in their heart. Their hearts had merged into one and, in the emerging, were steadily building in intense, pleasurable energy they had never felt before. They were holding each other in intensity, breathing into this heart energy. It was in the elation of love, a divine surprise. As they were melting into their merged heart, all went orgasmic; an orgasm shared, not two separate orgasms, but one orgasm with sensation there are no words to describe.

The words "time" and "love" have no place in the same sentence; perhaps they shouldn't be in the same paragraph either.

Sequoia and Teuton lay on their sides, gazing into one another's eyes, taking in the sacredness of magical feelings, of magical presence, that follow the deepest expressions of love. With their passions explored and thoroughly expressed, it was now imperative to stay present, taking time to just be ... together.

There were no words, yet volumes were being said in the silence they were embracing. Comforts and awareness of their unity, which had been made through the physical union of their bodies, were being completely expressed and absorbed for deeply storing the energies of the experience, in their cellular and energetic beings.

Their legs were wrapped around each other, their hands slowly moving to enjoy taking in bare skin of their beloved ... something they had denied themselves for so long.

They couldn't part.

For Sequoia and Teuton, time had ceased to be, and concerns had no place to interfere with the sanctity of the sacred union they had entered together. Their hearts were full, more full and open and vulnerable and courageous than either of them had ever known before; indeed, their hearts had expanded and were merged not only with one another, but with the love of all existence. Sequoia reached over to touch the tear she saw in the corner of Teuton's eye, and they burst out, first with a giggle and then into laughter that become more and more uproarious, with the joy of finding themselves merged and melted with the one person who meant the most to them, the one person they trusted the most, the one person they would give their lives to, not by dying for the other, but by living and being there for each other, through whatever life's challenges might be.

Teuton and Sequoia were now fully and completely life partners, and they were reveling in their new status as lovers.

They appeared at the doorway to the flight deck with arms around each other, leaning their heads toward each other, with rosy complexions, eyes gleaming, and delightful smiles. It was Monique who first saw them from the jump seat, where she had been observing the pilots at work. When she stood and came to the pair to join them in a hug, it drew the attention of the pilots, and Saladin and Gabriel came to the doorway of the technical quarters. Scera's eyes met Sequoia's, and they winked at each other. Then Scera began to get out of her seat and motioned for Redbird to do the same. Soon Sequoia and Teuton were surrounded in a group hug.

The sublime energy of the new lovers was being celebrated and shared beautifully.

CHAPTER 12

———ᴠᴠᴠᴏᴏᴏᴇᴄᴏᴇᴄᴇᴏᴏᴏᴠᴠᴠ———

The flight to Galeao Air Force Base, on a peninsula twenty kilometers from downtown Rio de Janeiro, was uneventful. The Dreamliner was guided over to park next to another plane that looked just like it. Upon seeing this, Redbird commented over the intercom that they might be meeting up with another of C-Know's planes.

Teuton opened the port-side entry door to see a stairway being brought to the plane. A welcoming committee of people were gathered. Teuton called for Gabriel and Sequoia to join him in greeting the people on the ground. As they descended the stairs, Sequoia recognized three other members of C-Know. It was a welcomed sight indeed.

Hugs and handshakes were exchanged, along with introductions. The Brazilian contingency of C-Know was represented by Maritza, who said, "We have been waiting for you. Everyone here has been briefed about C-Know, including what we have on board our planes; they know that you come to assist with canceling out the radioactive fallout. You already have clearance.

"We have a group of people in our plane right now deprogramming themselves. Now we can deprogram twice as fast.

"You will love this," she added: "Serendipity is that healers and meditators have been holding an international convention here in Rio these last few days. We're including them in our work.

"Gather the remainder of your crew and come with us. We want to bring you up to speed."

She led everyone into the building, down a hall, and into a briefing room.

Dr. Amaral, a scientist in a white coat, led the meeting; he began, "I thank you all for being here. First, we will brief you on Brazil's radiological protection capabilities.

"In Brazil, as in all of South America, we have been concerned that we would be victims of radioactive fallout, since it would be unlikely we would be directly involved in nuclear war. Therefore, we established studies in nuclear technology, with equipment to research what we might do to protect our people. Of course, protecting our people also means protecting the planet.

"Through the years, we have researched technology to neutralize atomic radiation, to transform atomic radiation into another form, and to gather radiation and contain it.

"Our research has been conducted using small quantities of radioactive waste. As you know, containment and storage has been the approach around the world. We have been sharing this technology with others throughout the world. Had we been in Chernobyl, we believe we could have entirely contained the radiation from their accident. We had the technology at that time. We've improved it since then.

"Our transformation research has been more interesting, in that we have been able to transmute radiation into other forms; however, we have created what appears to be new elements for the elemental chart, and as most of you know, that means these elements could combine with other elements to produce compounds not known before. We need more time to work with these new elements before we release them from the lab. These elements are not radioactive at the moment, but tests should continue for the next hundred years before we know the possible side effects.

"That leaves our radiation neutralization research. We have been researching how to increase the rate of decay of the radiation. Radioactivity is in a nearly stable state of suspension, waiting for a command to change its state of being.

"This is much like when an animal is intensely frightened and freezes up. It can't move, it can't do anything when the fear becomes excessive. There has to be some kind of intervention to free the animal from its frozen state. Humans freeze up emotionally and can actually remain frozen indefinitely. Energy is energy. What applies to energy in one form indicates what to look for in another energy form.

"At one point in our studies, we could not objectively study particles of energy because they responded to the researchers, no matter how much they tried to avoid having an effect on the energy. We realized the key to what we needed to know may be found in humans. So we began to work with people who could command radiation to change. As we observed the change in radiation happening from their thoughts or intentions, we analyzed our test subjects' brainwave signals."

"First of all, we found our best subjects had extreme clarity of thought. This means there was almost no dissonance of radio waves or energetic impulses from scattered thoughts.

"This brings us to what C-Know has developed, the technology and equipment found on your planes. You may be just what is needed to free people of mental dissonance so they can convey pure intention, therefore directing energy concisely.

"Our best subjects are people who know they can cause things to happen through their intention. These people seem to have confidence. The next best group of people we have worked with are those who do yoga and forms of meditation that quiet their minds. When given an intention to focus their energy on, these people are quite successful.

"Our conclusion is that in focused intention, human beings have the strongest impact upon energy. If you are religious at all, this supports creation theories; however, it might change your beliefs about what a supreme being is."

Some shouting could be heard outside. Everyone became quiet, intent on listening to what was going on to determine if there was danger coming their way. Three men rushed in, interrupting Dr. Amaral. They motioned for him to move with them to the corner of the room, where they began whispering together. Dr. Amaral moved his hands and gestured with certainty as he spoke to the men in muffled tones. Then they turned and rushed out the door.

When Dr. Amaral returned, he told the group, "Please pardon us. It isn't every day we have a worldwide emergency. I've just been given news that our fighters have intercepted and destroyed two nuclear missile launching submarines just off our coast.

"So let me explain: I've told you about people we've worked with who are most successful in changing radiation. We have learned some important things in working with them.

"First of all, of course, it's about working with someone whose mind is quiet.

"Second, it is important for the subject to know, in as much detail as possible, what they need to do. Now when I say 'do,' I'm talking about something very subtle. So to help us with this, we have prepared a video we show to our subjects to give them a very specific address, so to speak, for the radiation we want to change. We don't just use the general concept of radiation. We don't want to eliminate the radiation from the sun, for instance. So our video gives people a concept of the radiation we want to change. Then they command only the energy we wish to address.

"So in the video, we simulate as much as possible the radiation we want to neutralize, so our workers aren't scattered but focus their intentions in the same way.

"Third, we give a simple and clear intention for everyone to use. Yes, people are allowed to use their individuality but what we want to achieve is a very precise and clear message, an energetic message, directing the energy of radiation. We want a very uniform message going to the radiation when there are a lot of people involved. We don't want to give the radiation a confused message.

"Now that statement sounds like the radiation has a personality, right? I'm not qualified to make that judgment. I do know what works best. So our video also suggests the intention for the subjects to focus on for the radiation.

"Fourth, we suggest several models from what our most successful subjects have told us. It seems there are several styles that work equally well, that fit different people's way of doing things. For instance, most people are very visual. They are very effective with seeing things in their mind's eye, seeing the radiation, and seeing it change; we've produced some excellent results that way. Other people can produce results through sound. As you can imagine, we separate these people into different rooms so they don't distract each other.

"Finally, we found that having a specific target is important. Let me say that a little better. Location, a geographical area, a certain place, or a certain condition is important. For instance, we might be focusing on the radiation being carried in the wind over the Atlantic Ocean. Once that radiation has been dealt with, we address the radiation that has fallen into the water. Then we would deal with the radiation on the islands of the Bahamas, for instance. It's a little bit like dusting a room, filtering the air in a room, washing the walls, and then cleaning the floor. Methodically focusing on the radiation is very effective."

Teuton spoke up, saying, "There's just one very important part of this to add: our unseen helpers.

"What are you talking about?" Dr. Amaral asked.

"Those who are not in bodies, not incarnate, for some unknown reason are not proactive with helping us, but they're waiting for us to ask them. They're also very literal, so it is wise to be conscious of what we ask and how we ask it. You've already got specific instructions worked out well. Have you been involving them in your work?"

"Are you a nutcase or a scientist?" the doctor snapped impatiently. "We're not talking about asking god to do things for us here. We're doing it and leaving god to be an unsubstantiated hypothesis. We get results. Who knows if you ever get anything asking some gods to do it? What nonsense!"

"Respectfully, sir," Teuton replied, "millions, perhaps billions of beings have been added to those who are available to help. Since the time construct isn't the same for them as us, we don't need to think about their state of being so close to becoming disembodied. It isn't our concern. They do have an immense interest in what we're doing. They want the earth experiment to continue."

"So you say there are ghosts we can ask to help us?" Dr. Amaral asked.

"'Ghosts' implies souls attached to lifetimes, not letting go. They are ill as souls between lifetimes is concerned. They are of no help at all. They can't even help themselves.

"What I am talking about is our energetic essence, that which is the individual expression of Oneness, that which cannot die, that was before the Big Bang."

"How do you know they're there?" Dr. Amaral asked. "What if it's just another thing people create a hologram of because they have so much need to have supernatural help?"

"Both exist. Because we're the creators as a combined whole, the individual expressions have the quality of creation too. Energy gets combined, at least temporarily, with whatever we're creating with our desires and beliefs.

"I admit, religions are insurance policies for after the moment of leaving an incarnation. So there are a lot of ideas about what comes after life. And there are a lot of holographic energy patterns created from these beliefs."

"Right, so how can you say there are invisible helpers?" Dr. Amaral pressed him further.

"For me, it is a number of experiments with personal experience that have reliably worked out well. Don't just believe me. I don't ask for that. Belief is a hindrance. I'll give you a model to experiment with. If it works out, and we get more help, more power, and you observe the experiment went well, you can try other experiments. We get the additional power, and those for whom this is unfamiliar get the results of your first experiment. Then you'll try other experiments. Then you'll have your own experience base, like I do.

"My interest is getting results," Teuton replied. "I'm not into territorial issues about who is qualified or who exists or not. I simply want to involve everyone without qualification."

"Then you can lead on this one, and I will experiment with you," Dr. Amaral concluded.

"Okay, we can process six to eight people an hour per machine," Teuton said. "With four machines on each plane, and five other planes on their way here, we can expand the number of people who will be optimum subjects quickly."

"Good," Dr. Amaral replied. "I will tell my people to start bringing people here from the Riocentro Convention Center."

At the Riocentro Convention Center, every effort was being made to provide for those working on dissipating the energy of radiation. Rooms and resources were being prepared. Busses were shuttling people between the airport and the Riocentro, with police escorts to move them as quickly as possible. The Brazilians were in emergency civil defense operations and selecting volunteers to help.

The crew of each plane was busily processing a line of people through the deprogramming process.

Sequoia and Teuton took charge of communicating with the unseen helpers. Maritza and the other members of C-Know group instructed people who were cleared of old energy bundles and deprogrammed on how to join in dissipating the energy of radiation.

At the Riocentro Convention Center, the remainder of the C-Know group was just beginning to practice after viewing the video Dr. Amaral told them about.

The presence, the electromagnetic field of the meditative workers, was building powerfully. There was a palpable radiance, a discernable feel in the air, and a subtle sound of "Aum." It was the most powerful event since Oneness decided to create the universe from unmanifest energy. This was the largest group of the original assembly joined together in the power of creation that had happened on Planet Earth.

Words cannot describe all that was unfolding in those moments. The damage of explosions and death could not be reversed.

Maritza met the incoming C-Know planes as they arrived at Galeao Air Force Base and debriefed their crews. Each crew had stories of synchronicities that put them all airborne and how they were able to use high altitude flight and overflying oceans to avoid the explosions that could have disabled them.

From the reports, it appeared the bombs were exploded in populated areas, even Asian islands in the South Pacific and Eastern Indian Oceans. All of Asia, Europe, the Middle East, North America, North Africa, South Africa, and Australia were bombed. It didn't appear to have a political or military motive.

The best hope was that all nuclear bombs were used up or disabled.

They avoided making up stories they couldn't yet validate with evidence. They wondered if some areas weren't hit because missiles were only engineered to fly from the United States to northern Europe and northern Asia. The nuclear submarines may have hit targets not within range of land-based missiles such as South Africa, Indonesia and the surrounding region, and southern Asia. Whoever caused the world to be bombed wasn't completely thorough, but most of the world's population was hit.

They didn't know how much of South America was spared. It would take some time to assess the damage in the world. The C-Know planes were perfect for this assessment, not needing to land and refuel, but their work of deprogramming people to help with calming and dissipating the energy of radiation was more important.

The bombers probably planned to keep themselves sheltered and emerge after some planned period of time, but that remained to be seen. Satellites were not targeted, so all satellite capabilities continued. Global positioning still worked. Engineers could work on tapping into satellite capabilities to explore the world's surface as the surface became visible.

People who were identified as good candidates to help neutralize radiation were flown in to Rio from throughout South America. The first priority was to protect areas not devastated by bombing and then move to the hot spots to stop further radiation from traveling to areas not hit.

Evidence showed that their work with radiation was effective. Not knowing how much effort would be needed to complete the job, rotations were established, with volunteer services to take care of the needs of those working with radiation. They were prepared to continue indefinitely until they determined that all the radiation had been neutralized.

The plan to take care of radiation workers included some recreation, exercise, and rest. Teuton and Sequoia were joined by others who were adept at working with unseen helpers. This freed them to be shuttled to a suite in a hotel near the ocean for rest and rejuvenation. The media informed other people how to contribute to the work, especially how to build and contribute energy through lovemaking.

After significant rest and time spent making love themselves, Teuton and Sequoia took a walk on the beach together. They treasured their closeness and communicated in telepathy, especially noticing everything they were deeply grateful for. They knew, as did others working on radiation, the power of gratitude to affect the energy fields. They knew gratitude to be an abundance magnet far more powerful than coming from a place of neediness. Abundance is of Oneness and neediness of separation, not recognizable by Oneness or abundance. Oneness full of abundance could only recognize itself, not illusions of lack, need, desperation, or despair. The people working on radiation knew the truths of this much deeper than just being able to say the words and remember the concepts that describe it.

While the destruction was part of reality, focusing on the destruction would not solve the problem. Noticing what there was to be grateful for in the situation not only made them aware of the resources available to them, it also attracted more energy to assist with improving the situation.

As Teuton and Sequoia walked on the sands, they noticed all they could. It kept them in the moment, where their gifts and abilities were active. They couldn't afford the luxury of thinking about possibilities not in their immediate presence. Except for using verbal communication, they also couldn't afford to be thinking with vocabulary, for it would take their attention away from the moment. They knew witnessing, watching, and observing without thinking was all they could do to contribute to a shift in the consciousness and lifestyles of how the earth would unfold, one moment at a time.

You are God also. You can choose and create whatever you want. We didn't say you are a little human, we said you are God. —Tobias